THE DIVINE ROMANCE
Tales of an Unearthly Love

Born in 1944, John Davidson has had a lifelong interest in mysticism. Graduating in 1966 from Cambridge University with an honours degree in natural sciences, he worked for seventeen years at the University's Department of Applied Mathematics and Theoretical Physics.

In 1984, he left the University to pursue independent interests, and since then has written a number of books, including a series on science and mysticism. The present book is the fourth in a series on Christian origins, following on from his ground-breaking work, *The Gospel of Jesus: In Search of His Original Teachings.*

DI005600

BY THE SAME AUTHOR

On Science and Mysticism

Subtle Energy (1987)
The Web of Life (1988)
The Secret of the Creative Vacuum (1989)
Natural Creation and the Formative Mind (1991)
Natural Creation or Natural Selection? (1992)

On Christian Origins

The Robe of Glory (1992)
The Gospel of Jesus (1995, revised 2004)
The Prodigal Soul (2004)
The Song of Songs (2004)
The Odes of Solomon (2004)

THE DIVINE ROMANCE

Tales of an Unearthly Love

John Davidson

cb
CLEAR BOOKS

© John Davidson 2004

First published in Great Britain in 2004 by
Clear Press Limited,
Unit 136, 3 Edgar Buildings
George Street, Bath BA1 2FJ
www.clearpress.co.uk

All rights reserved.
No part of this book may be
reproduced or utilized in any form or by any means,
electronic or mechanical, without permission in
writing from the Publisher.

Designed by Wayne Caravella and John Davidson
Typeset by John Davidson
Cover design by Jerry Goldie

Printed in India by Ajanta Offset

British Library Cataloguing in
Publication Data available

Library of Congress Cataloging in
Publication Data available

ISBN 1–904555–11-X

DEDICATION

To the divine Bridegroom

Let me be worthy of your bride chambers
that are full of light....
Let me see your Image, my holy Father,
which I saw before the world was created.

Manichaean Psalm Book *CCLXIII*, MPB *p.79*

ACKNOWLEDGEMENTS

This collection of stories and commentaries would not have been possible without the prior work of a number of specialist scholars.

The original translation of *The Virgin, the Harlot and the Bridegroom* (original title, *Expository Treatise on the Soul*) was made by W.C. Robinson (in *Nag Hammadi Studies XXI: Nag Hammadi Codex II,2–7*, vol. 2, ed. Bentley Layton; E.J. Brill, Leiden, 1989), and is reprinted by permission of E.J. Brill Academic Publishers, Leiden, The Netherlands.

The excerpts from *The Gospel of Thomas* were translated by Thomas O. Lambdin (in *Nag Hammadi Studies XX: Nag Hammadi Codex II,2–7*, vol. 1, ed. Bentley Layton; E.J. Brill, Leiden, 1989).

The Damsel of Light and some other passages are modernized extracts from M.R. James' translation of the *Acts of Thomas* (in *The Apocryphal New Testament*; Oxford University Press, Oxford, 1989 [1924]).

Passages from the Manichaean psalms and the Mandaean Prayer Book are modernized adaptations of the original translations, respectively, of C.R.C. Allberry (*A Manichaean Psalm-Book*, Part II; Kohlhammer, Stuttgart, 1938) and E.S. Drower (*The Canonical Prayerbook of the Mandaeans*; E.J. Brill, Leiden, 1959).

Joseph and Aseneth is a collated rendering of the translations of Jacques Issaverdens (*The Uncanonical Writings of the Old Testament Found in the Armenian Mss. of the Library of St Lazarus*; Armenian Monastery of St Lazarus, Venice,

1901), E.W. Brooks (*Joseph and Asenath;* SPCK, London, 1918), C. Burchard (in *The Old Testament Pseudoepigrapha,* vol. 2, ed. J.H. Charlesworth; Darton, Longman and Todd, London, 1983), and D. Cook (in *The Apocryphal Old Testament,* ed. H.E.D. Sparks; Oxford University Press, Oxford, 1985).

Excerpts from the *Odes of Solomon* are from *The Odes of Solomon: Mystical Songs from the Time of Jesus* (Clear Books, Bath, 2004) by John Davidson.

Biblical passages are drawn mostly from the *Authorized King James Version, The Jerusalem Bible* or *The New Jerusalem Bible.*

The precise sources of these and other excerpts are provided in the relevant notes and references.

I am also grateful to a number of friends who have been through the manuscript making various valuable suggestions, in particular, Yvette Beigel, Mousson Finnigan, Ed Kennedy, Penny and Errol Norris, Matthew Seal, Geoff Wade, and Elwanda Whitten.

CONTENTS

INTRODUCTION

The Divine Romance *is the second of three books concerned with the interpretation of ancient parables and allegories, the other two being* The Prodigal Soul *and* The Song of Songs.

E verybody loves a good story, especially those with a mystery or a riddle. The message of some of the greatest literature the world has known is expressed in parable or story form. These parables address the most basic needs of humanity, needs so fundamental to our existence, yet hidden so deeply within the recesses of our being, that they are generally unconscious or, at best, remain unarticulated. They concern themselves with the ultimate mysteries of our existence: What is man? Why do we live? How best can we face this mysterious experience we call life?

It seems understandable that answers to such ultimate questions must – by their very nature – always go beyond words. Faced with the Absolute, we are speechless. Yet being human, we want to hear the tale.

For the most part, we look to the great teachers of our ancient past to address these fundamental issues. This they have often done in the simplest way that we could under-stand – through stories that in their telling could at least hint of an understanding that cannot be caught in words. Stories that could point the way. Good stories, told around innumerable firesides, passing along from soul to soul the accumulated wisdom of mankind.

Such stories are of many types. Some, like *Aesop's Fables,* are simple tales in which nothing but the moral is meant to

be understood. Often, the nature of the story is fantastical
or mythological – involving speaking and scheming animals,
for instance. Other stories are a mixture of straight narrative, explicit spiritual or moral teaching, and allegory. The
early Christian *Acts of Thomas* and *Joseph and Aseneth*
belong in this category, and ancient Jewish writers have
understood parts of the Bible (such as the *Exodus* story) in
this way, too. Some stories are entirely allegorical, written in
a form or style in which every word or phrase is intended to
convey a particular meaning through the use of symbols,
images and metaphors. One of the best examples of such
allegorical writing is the poem known as the *Robe of Glory*
or the *Hymn of the Soul,* found embedded in the *Acts of
Thomas.* Many Jewish and Christian mystics and philosophers throughout the ages have understood the biblical *Song
of Songs,* as well as some of the other stories in *Genesis* and
Exodus, to be of the same genre. A number of the parables
of Jesus are also of a similar nature, like the parables of the
sower, the wedding feast, and the good Samaritan.

Jesus and many other great spiritual teachers have used
stories to convey their message, and *The Divine Romance* is a
compilation of five parables or allegories, drawn from the
gospels and other early Christian and allied literature.

The metaphors and images employed in ancient parables
occur repeatedly in mystic literature. In fact, they constitute
a timeless language of metaphor used by writers of many
cultures, languages and times. Living Water, the Tree of Life,
the Bread of Life, the Bridegroom, the Bride, marriage, the
serpent, the pearl and the garment of the soul, for instance,
along with many other metaphors, are all commonly
encountered in the mystic literature of the ancient Middle
East. Some of these even date back to Sumerian times of the
third millennium BC.

The Western mind, usually unfamiliar with this style of
allegorical storytelling, has a tendency to take allegories
literally, as with the *Genesis* creation myths. But, as we will
see, that was not the way that many people of ancient times

actually understood them. Nor does it appear to have been the meaning their original writer intended to convey.

The essence of all the stories in this series of three books is a spirituality that is universal in character and common to all religions. In any open-minded study of the world's mystic and sacred literature, one is inescapably impressed, not so much by their diversity as by the common threads that unite them all. It is true that if we look at the variety of human interpretations, at the external trappings of the religions that claim these writings as their own, at the differences in the linguistic or cultural modes of expression, or at any other of their more outward features, we can find differences enough. But if, dispassionately, we examine the fundamental principles being voiced, we cannot help but note that they are all, essentially, saying the same thing. They all contend that there is one God, or one ultimate Reality. They also indicate that this Reality can be found and experienced within every individual in an utterly transcendent and indescribable mystic experience.

In early Christianity, this experience was called 'gnosis' – implying knowledge or experience of God. To attain this experience of salvation, the 'gnostic myth', as it has been called, always spoke of the need of a Saviour or Master. No one disputes this. It is clear that Simon Magus, Basilides, Valentinus, Bar Daisan, Mani and many other gnostics of that period all taught this basic principle. Indeed, it is probable that Jesus did so too, though with the passage of time his teachings have been greatly distorted. In modern times, this 'gnostic myth', regarded at a safe distance from across the centuries of history, has been studied critically as an interesting philosophy of long ago. But it seems to me that the essence of it is as true and relevant nowadays as it was then.

The 'gnostic myth' is the oldest story ever told – the story of the soul's separation from its eternal home with the Father, its wanderings in the labyrinth of creation, its follies and its heartaches, its eventual rescue by a divine Messenger, and its final return.

Echoes and variations of this story are found in the myth-ology, folklore and mystical allegories of every culture. It is a captivating tale that touches the spiritual heart, awakening memories of a peace and inner comfort long forgotten, stirring up a longing for the pure realms of being, beyond the strife and turbulence of the material universe.

It is the parable of the prodigal son, the prince who awakens the sleeping beauty, or the princess who has fallen under the spell of an evil power and awaits the touch and mystic kiss of the ever youthful and life-giving prince before her release can be effected. It is the story of the good Samaritan or *The Virgin, the Harlot and the Bridegroom.*

In one way or another, this story will always be told, for souls – having long ago left their home – will never be happy in the material realms. The soul, separated from its divine Source, is ever restless, finding no peace until reunited with its divine essence.

There have always been souls who have been called to make the journey home. And there have always been divine Messengers, Sons of God, Saviours or perfect Masters who have been sent to guide such souls on their long journey homewards. Indeed, it is this divine Beloved, calling from hidden places in the inner realms of light, who awakens the soul and fills it with the desire to find God, its source of being. But at the outset, the soul does not know who it is that is beckoning – or even that it is being drawn. Like a man waking from a deep slumber, he does not know that there is someone else who is awakening him.

In many places, I have relied upon the existence of my earlier book, *The Gospel of Jesus* (1995, revised 2004), to support the interpretation of particular metaphors. This is useful because it avoids making unsubstantiated assertions on the one hand, or burdening the text with extensive quotations on the other. Only if particularly beautiful or pertinent, or when they have not been covered in *The Gospel of Jesus,* have I included quotations in addition to those comprising the parable or story under discussion. Likewise, the various ancient texts used are generally described more fully in *The Gospel of Jesus*, and background details concerning them may be found there for those who are interested.

Regarding translations of the various ancient texts, I have generally relied on existing translations. There are a few occasions, however, when the intended mystic meaning seems clear, but it has not been adequately conveyed. Sometimes, the simple capitalization of a word makes all the difference. God, for example, could not be expected to have manifested the creation with a human 'word'. But if we write 'Word' – meaning his creative Power or Emanation – we have a statement with which mystics throughout the ages would all agree.

In instances of this sort, I have taken the liberty of either very lightly editing the text, or of adding explanatory words in parentheses. But no editing has been done unless the meaning of the full context supports it. I have also modernized archaic English. In some cases, where a number of scholarly translations are available of some particular text, I have combined them, indicating this by a reference to the various sources consulted. Also, because of the variety of typographic styles found in the many quotations, I have standardized the layout, as well as the spelling and punctuation. The aim has always been to help convey meaning with clarity, lucidity and simplicity.

Unless otherwise noted, any significant clarifications or additions to a translation offered by myself or the original translator have been placed in round brackets, while significant conjectured words or phrases, usually provided by the original translator to fill gaps in an original, defective manuscript, appear in square brackets ([ ]). Where translations used have been edited for any of the above reasons, this is indicated by the use of *cf.* in the source reference.

⁓

The Story so Far

The first book in this series, *The Prodigal Soul,* contains a number of parables and stories centred around the themes of the soul's departure from God, its troubles and its heart-aches while exiled in the creation, and its eventual rescue and return home with the help of a mystic Saviour. In this context, a Saviour is one who is united to God's creative Power -- the Word or *Logos.* At both human and higher levels, he is a manifestation, an incarnation or a personification of the Word. This is the essential reality of both the Saviour and the soul, and indeed of everything else in creation.

The Divine Romance continues this story, focusing in particular on parables and allegories that speak of the soul's spiritual 'marriage' or union with the Saviour and with God. In this imagery, the soul is the bride or lover, while the Saviour is the Bridegroom or the Beloved.

Characteristic of mystic literature, these parables often convey both an outer and an inner meaning. Externally, the bride is the devotee, the soul in human form, while the Bridegroom or Beloved is the Saviour, also as a living human being. Internally, the bride is the soul who has escaped from the body by means of spiritual practice, also called contem-plation, recollection or interior prayer. And the Bridegroom is the spiritual or radiant form of the Saviour, whom the soul meets on the inner planes.

So significant is this meeting, so poorly is it often under-stood, and so frequently does it appear in this collection of stories and throughout mystic literature, that it is worth devoting a little space to it here.

As all mystics have described, in one way or another, the soul and mind are held down in the body through the human imperfections or weaknesses of the mind. These result in its attractions and desires for the things of the physical senses and for involvement in material affairs. There is a reason for this. In a perfectly balanced human being, the soul dominates the mind, and the mind controls the senses.

In most of us, however, the soul is dominated by the mind, and the mind is uncontrollably attracted to the senses.

In a human being, the headquarters, so to speak, of the soul and mind are located in the head. This is more or less self-evident. It is injury to the brain, for example, that impairs mental function, rather than injury to the knees or any other part of the body. The mind and soul, however, are so intertwined that it is impossible at the human level to truly determine which is which. They manifest in a general way as our personal attention and consciousness.

Mystics say that this attention or consciousness has a natural focus at a centre between the two eyebrows. It has been called the third eye, the eye centre, the single eye, and by many other names, in many languages. However, it is not a physical centre, but a mental or subtle centre, and it is to this point that a practitioner attempts to withdraw his or her attention during spiritual practice. This is the first goal of spiritual practice or interior prayer.

When the attention of the mind and soul are fully withdrawn from the world and from the body, when they have focused completely at the single eye, then the attention need travel only a little further inward before the soul and mind leave the body altogether. This is effectively the process of death, of dying while still living in the body. This is what it means to 'die while living'.

The soul now passes out of the body and enters the lowest of the inner heavenly realms, which some writers have called the astral realms. And there, on the threshold of the inner worlds, the disciple meets the radiant or spiritual form of the Master. Like the physical form, the astral form is a projection of the Word. In fact, at whatever level the disciple reaches, the Master takes an appropriate form, in order to be with the soul of the disciple, as a guide. But the essence of this form is entirely that of the Word.

If the disciple has found the physical form to be beautiful beyond all other human forms, that is nothing compared to the light, the beauty, the radiance and the love that surround and emanate from the Saviour as he is seen on the inner planes. From this point onwards, the disciple knows from experience that he is never alone. He gazes at the Master with utterly rapt attention. He can seek and receive any guidance he desires. He can ask any question, communicating mind to mind and soul to soul. He is utterly content and enfolded in divine love and bliss. There is nothing that can compare with this experience, and it is the longing for this meeting that ultimately drives and draws a disciple to attend ardently to spiritual practice. As he rises up through the body towards this point, he realizes increasingly that the Master is always with him. Yet the veil of his own mind still lies between. But when he meets that radiant form of light, then he sees face to face.

There is no greater longing that can strike a soul than the longing to find God within. This indeed is the only true longing or desire in creation; all others are poor copies. It is a homesickness to overshadow all yearnings, a divine nostalgia that grips the soul and will not let it rest until the goal is reached.

But for an individual held captive in this world, who only has a vague idea of what God is like, this longing begins as a longing to be with his Master. The longing starts in this world. However much one may have longed to be with another person, it is only a dim and distant reflection of the longing of a loving disciple to be with his or her Master. But as the love for the physical Master matures, and the devotee's spirituality awakens and develops, so too does the longing grow to see the Master on the inner planes. And since such divine longing is inwardly inspired by the Master, then, naturally, the intention is that it should be answered.

It is this inner, spiritual form of the Saviour that is often referred to as the Bridegroom or the divine Beloved, and – in addition to more general mystic themes – *The Divine Romance* tells the story of the soul's love for and longing to meet this radiant form.

ONE

The Wedding Feast

$\mathbf{M}$arriage is normally considered one of the most important events in a person's life. It signifies the union of
two people in one of the closest of all human relationships.
For this reason, mystics of all times and places have
commonly used images associated with human marriage as
metaphors for the divine union of the soul with God. Jesus
was no exception, and his parable of the wedding feast has
some interesting features that spring to life when considered
mystically.

The parable is found in three variant versions in Matthew,[1]
Luke[2] and the gnostic *Gospel of Thomas*.[3] But it is probable
that none of these represent the original parable – though
Jesus himself may have told the same parable differently on
different occasions. According to Matthew, Jesus begins:

> The kingdom of heaven is like a certain king, who arranged
> a marriage for his son, and sent out his servants to call them
> that were bidden to the wedding: but they would not come.
>
> Again, he sent out other servants, saying, "Tell them that
> are bidden, 'Behold, I have prepared my dinner: my oxen
> and my fatlings are killed, and all things are ready: come to
> the marriage.'"
>
> *Matthew 22:2–4; cf. KJV*

The "king", the ruler of the land, represents God, the
supreme Monarch of all creation. His "son" is the Word or

Logos, the "Only-begotten Son",[4] the primary, creative emanation of the Father. The "servants" are the mystics, prophets, Masters or Saviours who are sent by God to call "them that" are "bidden" – souls incarnate in human form – "to the wedding". All human beings, by virtue of their human birth, are "bidden to the wedding" of the king's son. Everything unique concerning the human form arises from our potential to realize God. This is God's invitation to all human beings. But "they would not come":

> But they made light of it, and went their ways, one to his farm, another to his merchandise.
>
> *Matthew 22:5, KJV*

They do not understand the importance of the divine invitation inherent in being born as a human being, and they remain involved in material affairs. They all "went their ways". One is involved in "his farm" and another in his business, "his merchandise". Their response is found in a more detailed form in Luke, in whose version only one servant has been sent:

> And they all with one consent began to make excuses. The first said to him (the servant), "I have bought a piece of ground, and I must needs go and see it: I beg you to excuse me."
>
> And another said, "I have bought five yoke of oxen, and I go to prove them: I beg you to excuse me."
>
> And another said, "I have married a wife, and therefore I cannot come."
>
> *Luke 14:18–20; cf. KJV*

Or, as it appears in the *Gospel of Thomas:*

> He (the servant) went to the first one and said to him, "My master invites you." He said, "I have claims against some merchants. They are coming to me this evening. I must go and give them my orders. I ask to be excused from the dinner."

He went to another and said to him, "My master has invited you." He said to him, "I have just bought a house and am required for the day. I shall not have any spare time."

He went to another and said to him, "My master invites you." He said to him, "My friend is going to get married, and I am to prepare the banquet. I shall not be able to come. I ask to be excused from the dinner."

He went to another and said to him, "My master invites you." He said to him, "I have just bought a farm, and I am on my way to collect the rent. I shall not be able to come. I ask to be excused."

Gospel of Thomas 64, NHS20 pp.76–77

Everyone is so absorbed in the mundane affairs of life, which create the illusion of pressing importance, that the greatest opportunity of all time – being invited to the wedding of the king's son – is passed over without a second thought in favour of personal and material considerations. Matthew's version continues:

And the remnant took his servants, and treated them spitefully, and slew them.

Matthew 22:6; cf. KJV

In every world religion, mystics and prophets – the "servants" – have been badly treated during their own lifetime, even extending to their murder or execution, though many have subsequently been venerated as great holy men by future generations. Judaism and Christianity are not the only two religions with a history of persecuting saintly people while they lived and worshipping them after their death.

But when the king heard of it, he was angry: and he sent forth his armies, and destroyed those murderers, and burned up their city.

Matthew 22:7; cf. KJV

This is a passage unique to Matthew, fitting well with the apocalyptic and eschatological overtones of his gospel. Possibly, it is an insertion to the original parable; but the destruction wrought by the king can also be explained metaphorically as the soul's rebirth in this world, where the "city" of the body is burned up by the "armies" of human passions.

> Then said he to his servants, "The wedding is ready, but they that were bidden were not worthy."
>
> *Matthew 22:8; cf. KJV*

In any event, such souls are "not worthy" to come to the marriage of the king's son, for their minds are too impure, being darkened with material desires. As Jesus concludes, according to the *Gospel of Thomas:*

> Businessmen and merchants will not enter the places of my Father.
>
> *Gospel of Thomas 64, NHS20 pp.78–79*

Matthew's version of the parable continues:

> "Go therefore onto the highways, and as many as you can find, bid them to the marriage." So those servants went out onto the highways, and gathered together all as many as they found, both bad and good: and the wedding was furnished with guests.
>
> *Matthew 22:9–10; cf. KJV*

The king therefore opens up the wedding to everybody. The important and wealthy people of the world, too busy building the illusion of self-importance to realize the real nature of the offer they have turned down, are passed over in favour of the ordinary man, the humble man in the street, who struggles through life just trying to get along as best he can.

When mystics come, the majority of their disciples are drawn from the simple everyday folk of the world. Those who think they are 'somebody' are usually too full of themselves to even contemplate the idea of following a mystic or a spiritual path. They think that the idea is sheer folly or they are afraid of what their friends, colleagues or family will say. But people who realize that they are victims of life's processes and are not overly full of their own ideas concerning everything are more likely to be attracted to a mystic. Consciously or unconsciously, they recognize that there is something more to life than mere physical existence and the acquisition of material benefits. In Luke, the parable at this point reads:

> Then the master of the house being angry said to his servant, "Go out quickly onto the streets and lanes of the city, and bring in the poor, and the maimed, and the halt, and the blind."
>
> And the servant said, "Lord, it is done as you commanded, and yet there is room."
>
> And the lord said to the servant, "Go out onto the highways and hedges, and compel them to come in, that my house may be filled."
>
> *Luke 14:21–23; cf. KJV*

The meaning is the same. The self-righteous are excluded while the simple, the humble and the poor are invited. The "poor, and the maimed, and the halt, and the blind" are those who are spiritually destitute, spiritually incapacitated and spiritually blind. On receiving the invitation to visit the king's house, many realize its importance and value, and come willingly. Some, however, are brought to the marriage party by 'force'. In Luke's version, the king says: "compel them to come in". Something drives them from within themselves to follow the spiritual path, even though there may also be a powerful contrary urge in them.

And when the king came in to see the guests, he saw there a
man who was not wearing a wedding garment. And he said
to him, "Friend, why have you come here without a
wedding garment?" And he was speechless. Then said the
king to the servants, "Bind him hand and foot, and take
him away, and cast him into outer darkness; there shall be
weeping and gnashing of teeth."

Matthew 22:11–13; cf. KJV

When all these souls are called to the wedding, not all are
permitted entry. A soul must possess its own "wedding
garment", its robe of glory or natural purity and spirituality,
before it can come into the king's presence, into the presence
of God. The need for a metaphorical interpretation of this
passage is highlighted by the fact that none of the people
called in off the street could justifiably have been expected
to have arrived dressed for a wedding. The "wedding garment",
however, is inner – the "garment" of the soul, which bears
no relationship to outer clothes, whether they are osten-
tatious and grand, or torn and bedraggled.

Being cast into "outer darkness" where there is "wailing
and gnashing of teeth" is a characteristic ending to Matthew's
presentation of Jesus' parables. The "outer darkness" refers to
this world, where there is continuous suffering and misery
of all kinds – "wailing and gnashing of teeth".[5] Jesus then
concludes with a saying also used to end the parable of the
labourers:[6]

For many are called, but few are chosen.

Matthew 22:14; cf. KJV

There is a double meaning here. Firstly, it means that many
souls are invited to the mystic marriage by virtue of being in
the human form. But few are chosen at any one time to
tread the mystic path back to God. Others have to face the
sufferings of rebirth again.[7] It also means that many souls
may be initiated by a Master, but not all of them will be able
to realize God or even to gain release from birth and death

in just one lifetime. All kinds of people are attracted to a mystic. They are "called". But some are entirely devoted to their spiritual practice, while others are unable to relinquish their attraction to the things of the world. Ultimately, they will all be "chosen", they will all return to God; but some may have to be reborn before this can be accomplished.

Turning to the early Christian texts to see how this parable and its metaphors were understood in those days, we find numerous passages which refer to the "wedding garment"[8] and the "wedding feast". In one of the last speeches of Judas Thomas in the *Acts of Thomas,* for example, alluding to many of the parables of Jesus, the apostle says:

> I was bidden to the supper and I came,
> > and I refused the land and the yoke of oxen and the wife,
> > that I might not for their sake be rejected.
> I was bidden to the wedding,
> > and I put on white raiment,
> > that I might be worthy of it,
> > and not be bound hand and foot,
> > and cast into the outer darkness.
>
> > > > *Acts of Thomas 146; cf. ANT pp.428–29*

In other places, the marriages of this world are compared to the divine marriage, the eternal union of the soul with God. Judas Thomas, for instance, contrasts the physical marriage with

> that incorruptible and true marriage.
> And you shall be therein groomsmen entering
> > into that bride chamber
> > which is full of immortality and light (*i.e.* eternity).
>
> > > *Acts of Thomas 12; cf. ANT pp.369–70*

In another passage, one of the characters makes a similar comparison:

That time required its own (space), and is gone,
    now this time requires its due.
That was the time of the beginning,
    this is the time of the end.
That was the time of the temporal life,
    which passes away.
This is the time of the life everlasting.
That was the time of transitory joy,
    this is the time of the eternal joy,
    which passes not away.
That was the time of day and night,
    this is the time of day without night.

That marriage feast:
    you see how it has passed away and is gone.
But this marriage feast shall never pass away.
That was a marriage feast of corruption,
    this is a marriage feast of life everlasting....
That marriage gift was money and clothes,
    which decay and pass away.
This marriage gift is the Living Word,
    which never passes away.

        Acts of Thomas 124; cf. AAA pp.261–62, ANT p.419

And again:

You stand in the temporal life,
    and have not seen the everlasting life.
You are troubled by the wedlock of corruption,
    and have not become aware of the true wedlock.
You are clothed with garments that decay,
    and long not for the garments of eternity.
You are proud of this beauty that vanishes,
    but care not about the unsightliness of your soul.
You are proud of owning a number of slaves,
    but your own soul from slavery you have not set free.

        Acts of Thomas 135; cf. AAA p.269, ANT p.423, MAA p.232

The events and happenings of outer life can be so pressing in their sense of importance that we pass all our precious days absorbed in mundane affairs. The inner spiritual marriage, to which we have all been invited, is passed over in favour of our daily, external activities. Loves of the world take precedence over the love of the divine.

There is no doubt that the wedding to which Jesus refers is the mystic wedding and, as in the above, there are a great many places where the "wedding garment", the "garment", the "raiment", the "robe" or the "robe of glory" is also given a specifically mystic meaning. It is one of the most frequently encountered metaphors in the literature of the period, especially in gnostic writings. Alluding to the parable of the wedding feast, for instance, the writer of the *Gospel of Philip* says that no one can "go in to the King", can merge into God, without his divine garment:

> No one will be able to go in to the King if he is naked.
>
> *Gospel of Philip 58, NHS20 pp.156–57*

In the *Trimorphic Protennoia,* the author – following a literary style of the times – writes in the name of the Father. The soul is invited into the presence of God where it will receive its royal robes and "become gloriously glorious", as it was before it left the Father. The "Baptists", "those who give glory", "those who enthrone", and "those who give robes" are all references to the Saviours or Masters:

> I am inviting you into the exalted, perfect Light.
> Moreover, as for this (Light), when you enter it,
>   you will be glorified by those who give glory,
>   and those who enthrone will enthrone you.
> You will accept robes from those who give robes,
>   and the Baptists will baptize you,
>   and you will become gloriously glorious,
>   the way you first were when you were light.
>
> *Trimorphic Protennoia 45, NHS28 pp.422–23*

The Mandaeans, too, used the metaphor extensively. In a passage where eternity is the "place" or "house of Life", the soul is exhorted:

> Take, put on your garment of radiance,
>   set on your living wreath!
> Bow yourself! and worship! ...
> Praise the place of Life to which your fathers go....
> Good one (soul)! Rise to the house of Life,
>   and go to the everlasting abode!
>
> *Mandaean Prayer Book 92; cf. CPM p.96*

The Manichaean psalms also make frequent use of the term, as in an extract where the Saviour promises to lead the soul to the eternal realm, the "blessed abode":

> You shall rejoice in gladness, in blissful praises,
>   and you shall be without grief
>   and [...] forgetful of wretchedness.
> You shall put on a radiant garment,
>   and gird on light,
>   and I shall set on your head
>   the diadem of sovereignty....
> I shall set open before you the gates in all the heavens,
>   and I shall make smooth your path,
>   free from terror and vexation.
> And I shall take you with might,
>   and enfold you with love,
>   and lead you to your home, the blessed abode.
> And forever shall I show to you the noble Father
>   and I shall lead you in,
>   into his presence, in pure raiment.
>
> *Manichaean Psalms, Huwidagman VIc:3–4, Angad Roshnan VI:66–68*
> *cf. MHCP pp.101, 151, ML pp.86, 93*

In another verse, the writer says of such souls:

> They go to the heaven of light, ...
>> they receive as their nature,
>> the original splendour of the radiant palace,
>> and are joyful.
> They put on the resplendent garment,
>> and live forever in paradise.
>
> *Manichaean Text, SP p.915*

In another, the writer describes the peace and beauty of eternity:

> They are happy in the light and know no pain.
> All who enter there, stay for eternity,
>> neither blows nor torture ever come upon them.
> The garments which they wear,
>> none has made by hand.
> [They are clean and bright;]
>> nothing of the earth is in them,
>> (*lit.* no ants are in them)....
> Their verdant garlands never fade;
>> they are wreathed brightly,
>> in countless colours.
> Heaviness and drooping do not exist in their bodies,
>> paralysis does not affect any of their limbs.
> Heavy sleep never overtakes their souls,
>> deceptive dreams and delusions
>> are unknown among them.
>
> *Manichaean Psalms, Huwidagman I:18, 22–24;*
> *cf. MHCP pp.67–69*

It seems clear that in all these passages the "garment" of the soul is its own natural, innate splendour.

The Zoroastrian Connection

Imagery associated with the soul's "garment" goes back far earlier in ancient Middle Eastern literature than the gnostic writings of early Christian times. It can even be found in Zoroastrian literature. The third-century Iranian mystic, Mani, taught that Zarathushtra, whom the later Greeks called Zoroaster and who lived perhaps around 1500 BC, had also been a Saviour, a true Apostle – a divine Messenger sent by God to redeem those souls given into his care. Certainly, a study of Zarathushtra's *gathas* (poems) reveals that the essential elements of the mystic path are present in his teachings. Since Zoroastrianism was still a major religion in Iran and the surrounding areas in the time of Jesus and Mani, it is understandable that Mani and other mystics would have brought out the deeper meaning of Zarathushtra's teachings which had been obscured by the processes of religion. As Mani himself says in one of his works:

> Earlier religions (were correct) as long as holy leaders were in them …, but once the leaders had ascended, their religions became confused.
>
> *Manichaean Text, MM2 p.295, RMP a; cf. GSR p.216, GVM p.40*

There is no doubt that mystics use extant examples, parables, allegories, terms and expressions of past mystics that are in common use among the people to whom they are giving their teachings. A good example is the term *Vohu Mana*, often translated by scholars as 'Primal Mind', but used by Zara-thushtra for the creative Power of God, the Word or *Logos*. Almost two thousand years later, we find the term being used by Mani, with the same meaning, as the later Middle Persian variant, *Vahman*. In the Zoroastrian writings of the *Denkart*, *Vohu Mana* is described as "visiting" the soul:

Every opening of the (inner) eye
(comes to pass) by the complete visiting of *Vohu Mana*
to the life principle (the soul).

Denkart, CTPD p.281, in GVM p.46

Swedish scholar, Geo Widengren, also observes that *Vohu Mana*
is portrayed as the mediator between the soul and God:

It is related in a passage in *Datastan-i Denik* (a Zoroastrian
text) that the soul of the righteous man, accompanied by
the Good Spirit *(Vohu Mana)* who is the 'companion of the
soul' after death, ascends to the heavenly abodes and to the
garment.... And having introduced the soul to *Ahura
Mazda* (the Supreme Lord), *Vohu Mana* shows it its throne
and reward.

Geo Widengren, GVM pp.49–50

That is, it is *Vohu Mana*, the creative Power which takes the
soul to God and gives it its garment of light. In the same
Zoroastrian book, *Vohu Mana* itself is likened to a seamless
"garment":

It is necessary that it is the healthy, white, pure, single
(garment), made in one piece, just as *Vohu Mana* is in this
manner the first single creature (created power). Consequently, it is from him *(Vohu Mana)* that ... the innermost
and concealed garment has its appellation.

Datastan-i Denik 40:2; cf. GVM p.50

Again, in the Zoroastrian *Denkart*, reference is made to:

The light and white garment ...
(which is) the very selfness of *Ohrmizd (Ahura Mazda)*,
his garment and his brilliance.

Denkart, CTPD p.204, in GVM p.50

These passages all indicate that the garment of the soul is one with the divine essence, the creative Power or *Vohu Mana*, and that this was understood by Zoroastrian mystical writers of whom we know practically nothing at all.

In fact, many of the metaphors and parables, used in turn by Jewish prophets in biblical literature, by Jesus, by the Mandaeans, by Mani and by the many mystics or gnostics of the ancient Middle East, are traceable, historically, to Zara-thushtra. And before that, we find fragments of the same language of mystical expression on the clay tablets preserved for over 4000 years from the ancient Sumerian culture. In later times, the same metaphors were used by the great Sufis of Islam and the mystics of the East. Many people understand that mystic teachings are perennial, but it is surprising, too, how mystics use the same metaphors again and again, in different times and languages.

There is no doubt, then, that Jesus' parable of the wedding feast uses two of the most common ancient mystic metaphors to speak of the soul's return to God – the mystic marriage of the soul to God and the soul's innate garment of purity and light. These images occur repeatedly throughout the stories and parables related in this book.

NOTES AND REFERENCES

1. *Matthew* 22:2–14.
2. *Luke* 14:16–24.
3. *Gospel of Thomas* 64 (in *e.g. NHS20* pp.76–79).
4. *John* 1:14 (in *GJ* pp.509–13).
5. See also *Matthew* 8:12, 13:42, 13:50, 24:51, 25:30; *GJ* index: darkness, outer; *The Talents*, in *PSW* pp.29–30.
6. *Matthew* 20:16.
7. For a discussion of Jesus and reincarnation, see "Did Jesus Really Teach Reincarnation?", in *GJ* pp.406–60.
8. See *e.g. GJ* index: garment; robes; *The Prodigal Son*, in *PSW* p.13; *The Good Samaritan*, in *PSW* pp.18, 21–22; *Adam and Eve*, in *PSW* p.173; *The Robe of Glory*, in *PSW* pp.188–94, *passim*.

TWO

The Bridegroom

The soul's garment or robe of light, symbolizing its own pure spiritual light, is a garment possessed by all souls, if only we can find and wear it. But if this is true of unrealized souls, how much more so is it true of a Master, of the divine Beloved? It is no surprise, therefore, to find that mystic literature of all times and places contains numerous references to the light or spiritual form of a Master which is encountered by disciples on the inner planes. In fact, this is the first goal or major landmark in the spiritual life of a disciple. He comes to yearn for this meeting with the radiant form of his Master within himself.

Many people accept and understand that the soul's true nature is like a ray of light from the divine sun. From this, it is only a short step to realize that all souls, when they meet within, see each other as beings radiant with spiritual light. Likewise, a Master or Saviour when encountered in the heavenly regions is seen as a great being of light. He is a natural denizen of the realms of light, even while living in the body. And as soon as a disciple is able to step out of his body into these realms, he encounters his benefactor and Saviour in a spiritual form suited to those heavenly regions.

This form has been given many names in the mystic literature of the ancient Middle East, especially of early Christianity. It is the "angelic form", the "divine form", the "Likeness of light", the "Image" or *"Eikon"*, the "Dazzling One", the "Counterpart", the "Familiar", the "Twin" and the

"Pair-Companion". It is also the "Bridegroom" who is met with in the "bride chambers of light".[1]

It is in this form that a Saviour cares for his disciples. He is always within them, and can always be contacted there when the mind is sufficiently stilled, concentrated and purified. As Peter says, speaking of Jesus in the *Acts of Peter:*

> Though he be not seen with these eyes,
>   yet is he in us:
> If we will, he will not forsake us.
> Let us therefore purify our souls of every evil temptation,
>   and God will not depart from us.
> Yes, if we but wink with our eyes,
>   he is present with us.
>
> *Acts of Peter XVIII; cf. ANT p.320*

From his place within, the Master watches his disciple, seeing everything. He never leaves a disciple, but is with him to the end, purifying him of all past sins. He is very close, and can be contacted behind the eyes – in the twinkling of an eye.

A disciple's yearning for this meeting is expressed in many places in early Christian literature. In one of the Manichaean psalms, the devotee begs to see "your beautiful Image":

> Jesus, the light of the faithful, I beseech you,
>   do not forsake me.
> Your beautiful Image, my Father,
>   reveal it to me and your unsullied brightness....
> Let it arise and come unto me quickly....
> Reveal your face to me, O holy and unsullied brightness:
>   for you are my good Shepherd,
>   my true merciful Physician.
>
> *Manichaean Psalm Book CCLII; cf. MPB p.61*

With the passage of time, the spiritual meaning, especially of such esoteric aspects of mystic teachings, is easily forgotten or misunderstood. In Christianity, it seems clear that the passages in John's gospel where the author has Jesus describe the coming of the "Comforter" or Holy Spirit refer specifically to the disciples' inner meeting with the radiant form of Jesus. Jesus is very clear that this is a personal meeting between disciple and Master, taking place *within* the disciple, in the inner "mansions":

> Let not your hearts be troubled:
>> you believe in God, believe also in me.
> In my Father's house are many mansions:
>> if it were not so, I would have told you.
> I go to prepare a place for you.
> And if I go and prepare a place for you,
>> I will come again, and receive you unto myself;
> That where I am, there you may be also.
>> *John 14:1–3; cf. KJV*

And of that meeting, he says:

> On that day, you shall know that I am in my Father,
>> and you in me, and I in you.
>> *John 14:20; cf. KJV*

Then they will know from their own personal experience, rather than by faith and intuition, that he is really one with God, that he is within them; and that they will eventually attain union with him, that they will all become one. Jesus then speaks again of the disciples' meeting with his radiant form, this time calling it the "Comforter":

> And I will pray the Father,
>> and he shall give you another Comforter,
>> that he may abide with you forever;
> Even the Spirit of Truth; whom the world cannot receive,
>> because it sees him not, neither does it know him.
> But you know him,
>> for he dwells with you, and will be in you.
> I will not leave you comfortless: I will come to you.
>> *John 14:16–18; cf. KJV*

The "Comforter" is translated from the Greek, *Parakletos*, the Paraclete, which means Intercessor or Protector. This is the function of the Word, and its manifestation in the spiritual form of the Master. The physical Master will die one day, but the inner form will "abide with you forever". It is manifested out of the Word, the "Spirit of Truth". But this form cannot come to the people of the world, because they are not acquainted with the mystic Word of God. "But you know him," says Jesus, speaking of this mystic Comforter, "for he dwells with you, and will be in you."

Then he again assures his disciples – not the whole world – that although he may die and leave his disciples, physically, "I will not leave you comfortless: I will come to you." He will be with them and manifest himself to them in a higher form. Jesus is identifying his light form with the Holy Spirit, making it personal when he says, "I will come to you."

Mystics have often depicted the meeting of the soul with this divine Beloved as a divine marriage for, as the soul ascends, the two are increasingly united. The soul is like a bride who meets the divine Bridegroom in the bride chambers of the inner realms. This imagery is attributed to Jesus in a number of places in the canonical gospels. It also appears extensively throughout early Christian literature, and is commonplace in the writings of the later Christian mystics. It is the basis of the well-known parable of the Bridegroom and the ten virgins, five of whom were wise and five foolish:

> Then shall the kingdom of heaven
>   be likened unto ten virgins,
>   who took their lamps,
>   and went forth to meet the Bridegroom.
> And five of them were wise, and five were foolish.
> They that were foolish took their lamps,
>   and took no oil with them;
> But the wise took oil in their vessels with their lamps.
> While the Bridegroom tarried, they all slumbered and slept.
> And at midnight there was a cry made,

"Behold, the Bridegroom comes; go out to meet him."
Then all those virgins arose and trimmed their lamps.
And the foolish said to the wise,
  "Give us of your oil; for our lamps have gone out."
But the wise answered, saying,
"Not so; lest there be not enough for us and you:
  but go rather to them that sell,
  and buy for yourselves."

And while they went to buy, the Bridegroom came:
  and they that were ready went in with him
  to the marriage, and the door was shut.
Afterward came also the other virgins, saying,
"Lord, Lord, open to us."
But he answered and said,
"Verily I say unto you, I know you not."

Watch therefore, for you know
  neither the day nor the hour
  in which the Son of man will come.

Matthew 25:1–13; cf. KJV

If the Bridegroom is the Saviour, then the ten virgins must represent his disciples, half of whom are wise and half foolish. The lamp signifies the soul which has the potential to shine brightly, shedding light all around, as long as it is filled with oil to make it burn. The oil is therefore the spiritual practice which makes the soul shine brightly, burning in the fires of longing and separation from the Beloved.

All the disciples are expecting the coming of the divine Bridegroom. But only half of them make the necessary arrangements, by putting sufficient oil in their lamps. Only half the disciples ever attend to their spiritual practice in the way, and to the degree, that their Master has taught them. The others procrastinate, failing to make adequate preparation for his coming. They are lax in their spiritual practice.

While they await the Bridegroom, "they all slumbered and

slept" – they all slumbered in this world, outside the door, the single eye within which the Bridegroom is to be met. Then, at midnight, when the night is darkest, the Bridegroom comes and the ten virgins are called out to meet him. Midnight, when most people are fast asleep, signifies that disciples must be inwardly vigilant at all times, always holding themselves in readiness for the coming of their Master. It also refers to the night time when devotees stay awake in their spiritual practice, awaiting the appearance of their Beloved within.

The five wise ones are ready. They have kept oil in their lamps and the flames of their souls are burning brightly. With great joy, they "went in with him to the marriage" – they are taken through the inner door and merge into the Bridegroom on the inner planes.

But the five foolish ones are not ready. Despite the fact that they knew that sooner or later he was going to come, they had still permitted themselves to be distracted by the world – its pleasures, its pains and its activities. So they turn to their wiser sisters and ask for some of their oil. But in what may seem like an unkind gesture, the wise ones refuse, saying, "Not so; lest there be not enough oil for us and you." It means that spiritual wealth and spiritual practice is personal and cannot and should not be transferred, even if a person wants to do so. Each individual must go out and "buy for yourselves": everyone has to do their own spiritual practice. No one can do it for them.

So while the foolish ones are frantically trying to remedy their mistake at the last minute, the Bridegroom goes in with the wise virgins and closes the door behind him. And when the foolish ones come and knock upon the door, the Bridegroom refuses to let them in, declining even to know them. It means that they have wasted their opportunity of being in human form and of being the disciples of a Master. Since he has brought them into contact with the Creative Word, they will be given another opportunity in another birth; but in this birth, the door is shut to them.

Summarizing the parable, Jesus concludes: "Watch therefore, for you know neither the day nor the hour in which the Son of man will come." There is a double meaning here. Firstly, a disciple – being in darkness – cannot know how close he is to the opening of the inner door, when the Master will take him inside and meet him in his radiant form. Consequently, he must always endeavour to keep himself in readiness by concentrating fully at the inner door, remaining there in an attitude of genuine humility and love until the door is opened. If somebody is boring through a wall of unknown thickness, light only appears from the other side when the last millimetre has been broken through. Similarly, an individual cannot know until the goal is reached how close he or she has been to attaining it. Therefore, the effort must be maintained, whatever the apparent progress or lack of it.

Secondly, human life is fragile, and death can come at any moment. Since a Master in his radiant form will always meet his devoted disciples at the time of their death, this is also a time when such disciples can look forward to a meeting with him. But generally, no one knows when death will come. A person cannot presume that there is still plenty of time for spiritual practice, for one may expire very suddenly. "There is many a slip between the cup and the lip." Hence, Jesus says to his disciples, "Watch therefore" – stay alert and do not fall into the deep sleep of worldliness. Always continue with your spiritual practice.

There are many references in the early literature illustrating the mystic meaning of this parable, as in the Manichaean psalm:

> Let us also, my brethren, put oil in our lamps
>   until our Lord passes in.
> Let us not slumber and sleep until our Lord takes us across,
>   his garland upon his head, his palm in his hand,
>   wearing the robe of his glory;
> And we go within the bride chamber and reign with him,
>   all of us together.
>
> *Psalms of Heracleides, Manichaean Psalm Book, MPB p.193*

There are also many places where the devotee expresses a longing to be with the inner Master. One such psalm alludes to the parable of the Bridegroom, equating the vision of "your Image" – the radiant form – with the meeting in "your bride chambers":

> Let me be worthy of your bride chambers
>   that are full of light.
> Jesus Christ, receive me
>   into your bride chambers, you my Saviour....
> I am a maiden (devotee) unspotted and holy.
>
> Let me see your Image, my holy Father,
>   which I saw before the world was created,
>   before the darkness presumed
>   to stir up envy against your *aeons* (the eternal realm).
> Because of it (darkness), I became a stranger
>   to my (divine) kingdom.
> But now I have severed its root,
>   I have risen victoriously on high.
>
> Purify me, my Bridegroom, O Saviour,
>   with your Waters ... that are full of grace....
> [My lamp] shines like the sun;
> I have lighted it, O Bridegroom,
>   with the excellent oil of purity....
>
> Christ, take me into your bride chambers....
> Let me rejoice in all the bride chambers,
>   and give to me the crown of the holy ones.
>   *Manichaean Psalm Book CCLXIII; cf. MPB pp.79–80*

In another psalm, which also alludes to Jesus' parable of the good Shepherd, the devotee describes the meeting with the divine Beloved:

Christ, my Bridegroom, has taken me to his bride chamber,
  I have rested with him in the land of the immortal.
My brethren, I have received my garland.
My own land I have beheld, my Father I have found,
  the godly have rejoiced over me,
    my *aeons* have welcomed me.
My brethren, I have received my garland....

I am like a sheep seeking its pastor;
Lo, my true Shepherd I have found,
  he has brought me to my fold again.

Manichaean Psalm Book CCLIII; cf. MPB p.63

The *rendezvous* with this beautiful, radiant and spiritual form of the Master is the first goal to which the devotees on the mystic path aspire. It is without doubt that it is this meeting to which these early writers are referring in such passages.

Notes and References

1. For examples of the use of all these metaphors, see *GJ* index: radiant *or* light form of the Master.

THREE

The Virgin, the Harlot
and the Bridegroom

Origins

In one of the thirteen Nag Hammadi codices unearthed in the Egyptian sands in 1945, there is a short allegory or parable which tells the story of the soul. Its text, entitled the *Expository Treatise on the Soul*, or in the more popular title designated here, *The Virgin, the Harlot and the Bridegroom*, was almost certainly composed originally in Greek, but now exists only in the one Coptic translation. As with so many ancient documents, who wrote it and its place of composition are unknown. Its probable date of composition is towards the end of the second century AD.[1]

The author first narrates a simple parable concerning the fall of the soul and her return home. The soul is symbolized as a virgin who leaves her father's home and descends to the physical universe, where she becomes a harlot, taking many lovers. Her father (God) is not unaware of her plight, however, and when she repents, sincerely longing to return to him, he sends her a divine Bridegroom, who is also her Brother. Through him, the soul once more becomes pure and virginal, returning to her eternal and natural home.

After relating the simple outlines of the parable, its various elements are then discussed and embellished by the unknown writer, who supports his theme with citations from the Jewish scriptures, the Christian gospels, the letters of Paul and Homer's *Odyssey*.

The Virgin and her Divine Father

The parable begins:[2]

> Wise men of old gave the soul a feminine name. Indeed she
> is female in her nature as well. She even has her womb.
>
> As long as she was alone with the Father, she was virginal
> and in form androgynous. But when she fell down into a
> body and came to this life, then she fell into the hands of
> many robbers. And the wanton creatures passed her from
> one to another and [dishonoured] her. Some made use of
> her by force, while others did so by seducing her with a gift.
> In short, they defiled her, and she [surrendered her]
> virginity.

The soul is said, metaphorically, to be feminine because she
is the offspring of the divine Father, God, and is completely
dependent upon him for her existence. Her intrinsic nature
is that of love, devotion, surrender and of merging into the
divine Source. The soul is a drop of the divine Ocean of
Love, and her highest experience is that of merging back
into that Ocean. The meaning of the soul's "womb" is
explained presently.

When the soul is merged into the Father and is alone
with him, she is in her natural and innately pure and
virginal state. She is beyond the diversity, duality and
sexuality of the physical universe and can be said to contain
both sexes within herself, for she is one with the one Source
of all. She is thus "androgynous".

But when she takes birth in a physical body she becomes
subject to many "robbers" – the imperfections and passions
of human life – accumulating the debris of sin and karma.
Through the mind, she is attracted by sense pleasures and
worldly activities. Sometimes she is seduced by the allure-
ments of life and its transient events and comforts; sometimes her passions and lower tendencies overpower her and,
even against her better judgment, she behaves rashly. She

becomes engrossed in many ways in the play of material existence, losing her purity and virginity. Like a pearl that has fallen into the mud, she now appears dirty and defiled.

Human passions and the evanescent attractions of physical life have frequently been described as robbers and thieves in the mystic literature of the world, including the ancient Middle East.[3] They have likewise been called enemies, savages and wild beasts.[4]

> And in her body she prostituted herself and gave herself to one and all, considering each one she was about to embrace to be her husband. When she had given herself to wanton, unfaithful adulterers, so that they might make use of her, then she sighed deeply and repented. But even when she turns her face from those adulterers, she runs to others and they compel her to live with them, and render service to them upon their bed, as if they were her masters. Out of shame, she no longer dares to leave them, whereas they deceive her for a long time, pretending to be faithful, true husbands, as if they greatly respected her. And after all this, they abandon her and go.

The pure, virginal soul thus becomes like a harlot. She mistakes the love offered by the temptations of physical life for the only true love in existence, the divine love between the soul and God. There is only one Truth or Reality behind and within all the diversity of life. But under the influence of the mind and senses, the soul mistakes the outer reflection for the inner Reality. She seeks a faded counterpart of the true, divine love in the fleeting images and associations into which that pure love has been splintered and divided by the processes of creation.

The attractions of life, as well as the attachments to and demands of other people, are like "unfaithful adulterers". "Their word is stout, their performance lean."[5] They appear to offer comfort, solace, happiness and pleasure; but, since nothing lasts for very long, their outcome is unavoidable disappointment. Even a lifetime is a short period in the higher scheme of things. Since all things pass away in time or the mind gets bored with them, dissatisfaction is essentially built into all transient happiness and pleasure.

Understandably, the individual – comprised of soul, mind and body – gets frustrated. But being unaware of the real problem, we continue seeking one pleasure and activity after another, or one friendship after another, as each one fails to truly satisfy. Even if we endeavour to maintain relationships, the very processes of life can move us on from one thing or person to another. As a consequence, the people in our lives change as time goes by. Friends and associates of today pass out of our lives or even become our enemies, while family members are notoriously unpredictable in the attitudes they adopt. No one, however much they may be our well-wisher, can alter the course of our destiny, and their power to help us go through life is limited. Ultimately, death separates everyone, whatever the nature of their relationship.

The soul, therefore, "sighed deeply and repented" when faced with disappointment, satiation or boredom. But having forgotten her divine Father and her own naturally pure state, she does not know where else to turn, nor does she even realize the real nature of her problem. Consequently, through the habit of her mind, she turns once more to new 'lovers' or attractions. And "They compel her to live with them and render service to them upon their bed, as if they were her masters." The soul is entirely enslaved by the mind, and the mind by the senses. She is thus forced to maintain her intimate association with the mind and senses, and to serve them and their tendencies.

"Out of shame she no longer dares to leave them." Although somewhere deep within herself she realizes that there must be a better way of doing things, for the time being she can see no alternative. In her wretched state, she has no strength to turn to God for help or, if she does, she is struck by feelings of her own unworthiness and guilt. Like the prodigal son, she feels too low to even consider herself worthy to approach her divine Father.

Meanwhile, the events, vicissitudes and demands of life keep pressing in on her and, in her confused and distressed state, she is continually swept along from one thing to another. Yet every person and every attachment, "pretending to be faithful, true husbands, as if they greatly respected her", are eventually forced to abandon her, through the processes of life itself.

> She then becomes a poor desolate widow, without help; not even a measure of food was left her from the time of her affliction. For from them she gained nothing except the defilements they gave her while they had concourse with her. And her offspring by the adulterers are dumb, blind, and sickly. They are feeble minded.

So, ultimately, the soul is left alone and bereft, no one offering any genuine help or solace. "Not even a measure of food", nothing of any value, is left with her from her many encounters and experiences in life. From these she has "gained nothing except the defilements" – the load of sins and karma impressed upon her mind and weighing down her soul – which have been heaped upon her as a result of her many adventures. Her "offspring", the fruits of her association with the things and people of physical existence, have no life in them. She is emotionally exhausted, mentally confused, and her spiritual perceptions and understanding can best be described as "dumb, blind", "sickly" and "feeble minded". These are the fruits of her journey through material life. The soul has reached her lowest ebb.

> But when the Father who is above visits her, and looks down upon her, and sees her sighing – with her sufferings and disgrace – and repenting of the prostitution in which she engaged, and when she begins to call upon [his Name]

so that he might help her, [imploring him with] all her heart, saying, "Save me, my Father, for behold I will render an account [to you, for I abandoned] my house (spiritual home) and fled from my maiden's quarters. Restore me to yourself again." When he sees her in such a state, then he will count her worthy of his mercy upon her; for many are the afflictions that have come upon her because she abandoned her house (spiritual home).

When, through bitter experience of life in this world, the soul truly repents of her "prostitution", of giving her love and attention to all and sundry, and to every passing pleasure, then the Father – who is never unaware of what his daughter is going through – "will count her worthy of his mercy". When she begins to understand that she has left her eternal, pristine and natural home of spiritual purity, absorbed in the ocean of her Father, and has undergone nothing but suffering as a result, and when she wishes only to regain her original condition, then the Father has mercy on her.

The Prostitution of the Soul

This, then, is the simple parable, and the writer now begins a discussion of its various aspects, quoting biblical and other passages to elucidate his theme and to demonstrate that this teaching is neither new nor confined to any one particular culture or religion. In the process, he shows that many of the biblical narratives are to be understood as allegories or metaphors, and were not intended to be taken literally:

Now concerning the prostitution of the soul, the Holy Spirit prophesies in many places. For he said in the prophet Jeremiah:

If the husband divorces his wife, and she goes and takes
another man, can she return to him after that? Has not
that woman utterly defiled herself? "And you prostituted
yourself to many shepherds, and you returned to me!"
said the Lord. "Take an honest look and see where you
prostituted yourself. Were you not sitting in the streets
defiling the land with your acts of prostitution and your
vices? And you took many shepherds for a stumbling
block for yourself. You became shameless with everyone.
You did not call on me as kinsman or as father or
author of your virginity."[6]

Speaking metaphorically, God upbraids the soul for prosti-
tuting herself to her many lovers ("shepherds") in the
creation, and for never calling on the Father as her true
"kinsman" or as the origin of the purity she has so recklessly
squandered.

Again it is written in the prophet Hosea:

Come, go to law with (denounce, plead with) your
mother, for she is not to be a wife to me nor I a husband
to her. I shall remove her prostitution from my
presence, and I shall remove her adultery from between
her breasts. I shall make her naked as on the day she was
born, and I [shall] make her desolate like a land without
[water], and I shall make her [longingly] childless. [I]
shall show her children no pity, for they are children of
prostitution, since their mother prostituted herself and
[put her children to shame].

For she said, "I shall prostitute myself to my lovers. It
was they who gave me my bread and my water and my
garments and my clothes and my wine and my oil and
everything I needed."

Therefore behold I shall shut them up so that she
shall not be able to run after her adulterers. And when
she seeks them and does not find them, she will say, "I

shall return to my former husband, for in those days I was better off than now."[7]

In *Hosea,* following a literary custom of the times, it is God (Yahweh) who is 'speaking'. The book of *Hosea* begins with Yahweh 'saying' to Hosea, "the country itself has become nothing but a whore by abandoning Yahweh",[8] and the book itself speaks symbolically of Yahweh's marriage to the children of Israel as a marriage to a faithless wife. This is a familiar theme among the writings of the Jewish prophets,[9] where the children of Israel often symbolize the soul. The writer of the present story is presuming that Hosea is speaking allegorically. Likewise, the prophet Ezekiel devotes two long allegories to the same theme. It is from one of these that the present writer goes on to quote:

Again he said in Ezekiel:

"It came to pass after much depravity," said the Lord, "you built yourself a brothel and you made yourself a beautiful place in the streets. And you built yourself brothels on every lane, and you wasted your beauty, and you spread your legs in every alley, and you multiplied your acts of prostitution. You prostituted yourself to the sons of Egypt, those who are your neighbours, men great of flesh."[10]

But what does "the sons of Egypt, men great of flesh" mean if not the domain of the flesh and the perceptible realm and the affairs of the earth by which the soul has become defiled here, receiving "bread" from them, as well as "wine", "oil", "clothing", and the other external nonsense surrounding the body – the things she thinks she needs.

These ancient writers were clearly no prudes. They make their point in forceful language which they know will attract people's attention, something modern advertising companies have long since recognized. Throughout the ages, mystics have used sexual imagery to convey their teachings. The great Jalalu'ddin Rumi, a thirteenth-century Sufi mystic of Persia, uses such ribald language in parts of his great work, the *Masnavi,* that R.A. Nicholson, translating in the early twentieth century, felt constrained to translate some of these passages into Latin, rather than English. Such imagery has been prevalent in the mystic writings of the Middle East for more than two and a half thousand years, and the Old Testament contains many such examples.

The writer is saying that the "sons of Egypt" as opposed to the "children of Israel" are the people, things and affairs of the world. He is explicit concerning this. He says that the soul tries to take its sustenance from useless things of the world – the "external nonsense surrounding the body" – rather than from the Lord. Metaphors concerning Egypt generally refer to a mystic understanding of the *Exodus* story as an allegory concerning the captivity of the soul (the children of Israel) in this world (Egypt). According to the well-known legend, they are freed by a Saviour (Moses), fed with manna or Bread from heaven (the Word), and taken to the promised land (the eternal realm).

But as to this prostitution, the apostles of the Saviour commanded: "Guard yourselves against it, purify yourselves from it,"[11] speaking not just of the prostitution of the body, but especially of that of the soul. For this reason the apostles [wrote to the churches] of God, that such [prostitution] might not occur among [us].

Yet the greatest [struggle] has to do with the prostitution of the soul. From it arises the prostitution of the body as well. Therefore Paul, writing to the Corinthians, said:

I wrote you in the letter, "Do not associate with prostitutes,"[12] not at all (meaning) the prostitutes of this world or the greedy or the thieves or the idolaters, since (to do that) you would have to leave this world.

Here, he is speaking spiritually:

> "For our struggle is not against flesh and blood,"

as he said,

> "but against the world rulers of this darkness and the spirits of wickedness."[13]

The writer points out that the meaning of his parable and that of both the Jewish prophets and the apostles is spiritual. It is from this "prostitution of the soul" that the "prostitution of the body" arises, and this includes all other perversities and imperfections. Whatever is within is automatically reflected without.

He also quotes Paul who – according to this writer – equates the "prostitutes" with the "world rulers of this darkness" and the "spirits of wickedness". Commonly described in gnostic literature, these "rulers" are the *archons* or powers who administer this world ("this darkness") and the higher regions of the mind – the astral and causal realms.[14] They are the higher cause or blueprint of the human imperfections with which man struggles. Incidentally, Paul's comment also indicates that whatever else he may have believed and taught, he also had gnostic leanings.

The explanation of the parable continues:

> As long as the soul keeps running about everywhere, uniting with whomever she meets and defiling herself, she exists, suffering her just deserts. But when she perceives the straits she is in and weeps before the Father and repents, then the Father will have mercy on her, and he will make her womb turn from the external domain and will turn it again inward, so that the soul will regain her proper character. For it is not so with a woman. For the womb of the body is inside the body like the other internal organs, but the womb of the soul is around the outside....

So when the womb of the soul, by the will of the Father, turns itself inward, it is baptized and is immediately cleansed of the external pollution that was pressed upon it, just as [garments, when] dirty, are put into the [water and] turned about until their dirt is removed and they become clean. And so the cleansing of the soul is to regain the [newness] of her former nature, and to turn herself back again. That is her baptism.

While the soul remains like a prostitute, profligately letting her attention spread out into the world, she suffers "her just deserts". According to the law of karma or cause and effect, she has to reap whatever she has sown. But when she truly realizes the "straits she is in" and genuinely wishes to remedy matters, then the Father himself extends his grace and brings about a reversal of the direction of the mind. This is true repentance. But it comes about more by the grace of God than by the efforts of the individual. The seeming efforts of the individual are actually a response to the grace or pull of the Father.

Here it becomes clear that the "womb" of the soul is its external covering of the mind, full of "external pollution". It is the Father who turns the direction of this covering inwards. And he does so by means of a "baptism" that cleanses the dirt from the soul's coverings, permitting her to "regain the [newness] of her former nature" – to come to know her real, pristine and essential nature. A baptism which enables the soul to acquire mystic knowledge of her real self is clearly no physical immersion in the water of this world. It is an inner mystic retuning of the soul to the Creative Word of God, an immersion in the Living Water.

The Coming of the Bridegroom

The Father's response to the soul's longing is now described in greater detail:

Then she will begin to rage at herself like a woman in labour, who writhes and rages in the hour of delivery. But since she is female, by herself she is powerless to beget a child. So from heaven the Father sent her her man, who is her Brother, the First-born. Then the Bridegroom came down to the bride.

Inspired by divine grace, the soul begins to seek the path to God. But, of herself, she can find neither God nor even the path that leads to him. Just as a woman cannot give birth to a child without a man, so too is it impossible for a soul to find God without a Helper or Saviour. This Saviour, says the writer, is the "Brother", the "First-born" or the "Bridegroom". These were all common epithets, in those times, for a perfect Saviour or Master.[15]

The three names signify the forms in which the Saviour manifests. He is the "Brother" because he is manifested at the human level as a man. He talks with us, laughs with us, faces all the difficulties which we have to face, and behaves like a real brother or friend. When he appears in the heavenly realms of creation, he is the "Bridegroom". The term is an allusion to the imagery of the divine marriage of the soul (the bride) to the Saviour. But at whatever level the Saviour reveals himself, his real essence is the "First-born" or "Only-begotten" Son of the Father, the Creative Word. The Word emanates from God without the help of any intermediary, as the primal creative outpouring by which creation comes into existence. He takes a form – spiritual or material – only so that he may contact the soul.

The "Bridegroom", therefore, comes down to the "bride" who at this point is likened to a repentant harlot. The soul, of course, immediately responds to the coming of her eternal Beloved:

She gave up her former prostitution and cleansed herself of the pollutions of the adulterers, and she was renewed so as to be a bride. She cleansed herself in the bridal chamber;

she filled it with Perfume; she sat in it waiting for the true Bridegroom.

No longer does she run about the market place (of this world), uniting with whomever she desires, but she continued to wait for him – (saying), "When will he come?" – and to fear him, for she did not know what he looked like: she no longer remembers since the time she fell from her Father's house. But by the will of the Father [she comes to long for him?]. And she dreamed of him like a woman in love with a man.

She conquers her former passions and imperfections, and sets about preparing herself to become a worthy bride of such a Bridegroom. "She cleansed herself in the bridal chamber" refers obliquely to the single eye or eye centre, and to the practice of mystic prayer. In ancient times, details of actual spiritual practices were never written down in straightforward language. Metaphors were always employed. Jesus, for example, called this centre the "door", the "strait gate", the "eye of a needle", the narrow way or the single eye.[16] Situated mentally, not physically, between the two eyebrows, the single eye is the 'bedroom' of the soul and mind in the physical body.

From this point, the attention spreads out into the world through the senses. Each 'ray' of attention is a ray of the soul's love, for love is the only power that exists within the soul. But, by these 'rays', the soul has become enamoured of the world and its people, becoming like a harlot in the diversity and changeability of her lovers, the attractions of the world of the senses. Her pure love is misdirected and misused, becoming impure through the way she expresses it.

Therefore, to begin with, purity consists of withdrawing all the attention from the senses and stilling the mind at the single eye. It is purified of all external or sensory impressions and desires. This is like entering a bedroom or "bridal chamber", making preparations to meet the Bridegroom. The outer world is forgotten as the soul prepares herself for this encounter. From the time of mystic baptism, the Bridegroom or Master dwells within the disciple. By concentrating all the attention at the single eye and entering the "strait gate", the soul comes face to face with the astral, radiant or light form of the Master. In the ancient literature, as we have seen, this form is often called the Bridegroom.[17]

For as long as the soul, through the mind, entertains sensual desires of any kind, and for as long as the mind is still allured by thoughts of the world, for just so long will the soul and mind remain scattered and profligate, wandering around in the world away from the single eye. But as soon as the soul develops a one-pointed love and desire for the spiritual Bridegroom within, to the exclusion of all other thoughts and desires, then she is able to enter the bridal chamber and wait there in purity of being. It is necessary for her to wait because the Bridegroom only comes when he deems fit. The soul cannot demand his appearance as her right. He is, after all, a divine Bridegroom!

"No longer does she run about the market place (of this world), uniting with whomever she desires, but she continued to wait for him, (saying), 'When will he come?'" This is the state of longing, of an ever increasing intensity, which descends upon a soul as she waits for the spiritual form of the Master to come to her. The longing purifies the soul of subtle traces of egotism and worldliness, and she thinks and dreams of her Beloved at all times of the day and night.

The bride also fills her "bridal chamber" "with Perfume". "Perfume" or Fragrance is a common allusion in ancient mystic writings of the Middle East[18] to the divine Music of the Word, which the soul begins to hear when she concentrates at the single eye. It is the sweetness of this divine Music that ultimately captivates the mind, holding it at the single eye, preventing it from running out into the pleasures of physical existence. The mind is pleasure loving by nature. But the higher and sweeter pleasure of the divine Music or "Perfume" automatically detaches it from material pleasures in a positive, forceful and life-giving way which no ascetic practices, self-abnegation or mental introspection of any kind can ever do.

> But then the Bridegroom, according to the Father's will, came down to her into the bridal chamber, which was prepared. And he decorated the bridal chamber.

And when the "Bridegroom" comes, he comes "according to the Father's will". Nothing that a perfect Master does is outside of God's will, for he is one with his Father, as Jesus said.[19] Just as a marriage of this world requires the permission and blessings of the bride's father, so too does the spiritual marriage. The marriage of the soul and the divine Beloved – the Word or *Logos* – takes place entirely by the will of the Father.

So the "Bridegroom" enters the "bridal chamber, which was prepared". He appears within the disciple, the devotee, the bride, as she sits in concentration at the single eye during her spiritual practice. "And he decorated the bridal chamber" – he fills the devotee with the Perfume of the Word, which is his essence, and with the blissful nectar and atmosphere of his loving presence. This is spiritual 'decoration' of the mystic 'bedroom'.

> For that marriage is not like the carnal marriage, where those who have union with one another are satisfied with that union. And (afterwards), as if it were a burden, they leave behind them the annoyance of physical desire, and they [turn their faces from] each other. But this marriage [is different?]. For [once] they unite [with one another], they become a single life. Wherefore the prophet said concerning the first man and the first woman:
>
> They will become a single flesh.[20]

For they were originally joined to one another when they were with the Father, before the woman (Eve) led astray the man (Adam), who is her Brother. This marriage has brought

them back together again and the soul has been joined to
her true love, her real Master, as it is written:

> For the Master of the woman is her husband.[21]

The translation of the first paragraph is uncertain, but there
seems little doubt that the author is comparing physical
union with the spiritual. In a "carnal marriage", he says, the
partners remain separate, turning their backs upon each
other after the gratification of their desire, as if it had been a
"burden". But in the spiritual marriage, the soul is fired by a
continuous longing, and the union of the bride and
Bridegroom leads to a complete merging, such that they
become "a single life". They never wish to be apart from
each other. Bodies can never truly merge, the one with
another, making one body. It is only in the realm of the
Spirit that real unity of being is possible.

Then, taking another of the *Genesis* stories as an allegory,
the writer refers to the unity of Adam and Eve with the
Father, before their 'Fall', linking its meaning to a saying
paraphrased from *Genesis* and the letters of Paul. His meaning is that the true Bridegroom, husband, "real Master" or
Brother of the soul is her "true love". All other loves are false
and profligate.

> Then gradually she recognized him, and she rejoiced once
> more, weeping before him as she remembered the disgrace
> of her former widowhood. And she adorned herself still
> more, so that he might be pleased to stay with her.

When the Bridegroom, the light form of the Master, comes
to her, she realizes increasingly who he actually is, at the
same time becoming more acutely aware of her own imperfections. Consequently, "she adorned herself still more": she
tries har-der to purify and eliminate all the remaining traces
of egotism and attachment to the material world, "so that he
might be pleased to stay with her".

When the soul meets the Bridegroom on the inner planes, she finds that he does not always stay with her. He comes and goes, according to his own sweet will. The blissful, beautiful and radiant form of the Master, having engendered tremendous love in the soul, then plays a game of hide and seek with her in order to purify her of the last vestiges of imperfection through the fires of love, longing and separation. At times, he manifests himself to the soul, at other times he goes higher up, so that the soul has to gather together all her concentration and love, urged on by the longing to be with him every moment.

And the prophet said in the *Psalms:*

> Hear, my daughter, and see and incline your ear and forget your people and your father's house, for the King has desired your beauty, for he is your Lord.[22]

For he requires her to turn her face from her people and the multitude of her adulterers, in whose midst she once was, to devote herself only to her King, her real Lord, and to forget the house of the earthly father with whom things went so badly for her, but to remember her Father who is in heaven. Thus also it was said to Abraham:

> Come out from your country and your kinsfolk and from your father's house.[23]

To stay forever with the divine Beloved, the soul must entirely relinquish all mental attachment to the loves of her former life. The writer quotes from the *Psalms,* and also once again from *Genesis,* now taking a part of the story of Abraham allegorically. The soul must utterly abandon her physical attachments and associations, not externally, but mentally. She must be free within herself to give all her love and every part of her being to the love of the divine Beloved.

She must give up her "earthly father", "come out from" her "father's house" and "remember her Father who is in heaven". This requires great effort and is only accomplished by the grace of the Beloved.

> Thus when the soul [had adorned] herself again in her (own natural) beauty, [she loved and?] enjoyed her Beloved, and [he also] loved her. And when she had communion with him, she received from him the Seed that is the life-giving Spirit, so that by him she bears good children, and rears them. For this is the great, perfect marvel of birth. And so this marriage is made perfect by the will of the Father.

So the soul, the bride, experiences union with the Bridegroom, and the "Seed" that she receives from him is that of the "Spirit". She is initiated into the Holy Spirit, the Word. The Seed (the Word of God) and receiving the Seed (mystic baptism) are once again common metaphors in the mystic literature of this period, as in Jesus' parable of the sower and his divine Seed.[24]

The "children" which she bears as a result of this union are "good children", rather than the "dumb, blind", "sickly" and "feeble minded" ones of her former worldly lusts and entanglements. These "children" are purity of soul and spiritual progress. She hears the divine Music of the Word; she hears the Voice of the First-born Son of God; she is able to travel with her Beloved through the realms of the Spirit, ultimately reaching the Father himself. "This is the great, perfect marvel of birth" – of rebirth or being born again into the family of Life, the family of a Saviour who is the Word incarnate. Mystic baptism was often referred to as a rebirth, as in John's gospel and in many other places in the ancient literature.[25] Thus, "this marriage is made perfect by the will of the Father" – only by the Father's will does the soul return to him and attain perfection.

Now it is fitting that the soul regenerate herself and become
again as she formerly was. The soul then moves of her own
accord (is free). And she received the divine nature from the
Father for her rejuvenation, so that she might be restored to
the place where originally she had been. This is the
resurrection that is from the dead. This is the ransom from
captivity. This is the upward journey of ascent to heaven.
This is the way of ascent to the Father.

The soul recovers her own natural state, free from the mind
and all the encumbrances of the lower creation. She receives
"rejuvenation". She comes into contact with the Spring of
eternal life, the Word, and she is "restored to the place where
originally she had been" – her eternal, spiritual home with
the Father. She has been raised from the death of this world
and taken to the Source of eternal life. When the soul and
mind concentrate completely at the eye centre to the complete
exclusion of all other thoughts and sensory distractions, all
consciousness is withdrawn from the body. Then the soul
and mind actually leave the body and pass into the astral or
heavenly regions. This is the process of dying while living.
This is true "resurrection". It is resurrection "*from* the dead",
not "*of* the dead".[26]

The Master also comes and pays the soul's "ransom from
captivity".[27] The debt of sins or karma that weighs heavily
on the mind and is responsible for holding the soul down in
this world, in life after life, is repaid by the Saviour. He pays
the ransom on the soul's behalf so that she may go free. The
soul is therefore enabled to ascend to heaven.[28] She leaves
the body and travels through the inner heavens, back to the
eternal realm, the kingdom of heaven, where she finds and
merges into the Father.

Therefore the prophet said:

Praise the Lord, O my soul,
    and all that is within me,
        (praise) his holy name.

My soul, praise God, who forgave all your sins,
    who healed all your sicknesses,
    who ransomed your life from death,
    who crowned you with mercy,
    who satisfies your longing
    with good things (of the Spirit).
Your youth will be renewed like an eagle's.[29]

Then when she becomes young again, she will ascend,
praising the Father and her Brother by whom she was
rescued. Thus it is by being born again that the soul will be
saved.

The writer quotes the *Psalms* in support of his thesis,
demonstrating yet again that many of the biblical books, in
this case the *Psalms,* contain age-old and universal truths.
Forgiveness of sins as the payment of a ransom, physical life
being understood as death, the healing of spiritual sickness,
and the receipt of "good things" or spiritual riches are all
commonly encountered descriptions of spiritual truths.
They are found throughout the mystic literature of the
world. They are eternal and ever existent realities of the
highest kind of spiritual life. They did not come into
existence only with the advent of Jesus.

So the soul, rescued by her "Brother" – the Saviour or
Master in physical form – receives the mantle of eternal
youth. Through initiation into the Spirit, she is infused with
spiritual life, she learns to fly like an "eagle" and ascend to
the Father. It is by "being born again" into the Word that the
"soul will be saved".

And this is due not to rote phrases or to professional skills
or to book learning. Rather it [is] the grace of the [Brother,
it is] the gift of the [Father]. For such is this heavenly thing.
Therefore the Saviour cries out:

No one can come to me unless my Father draws him
and brings him to me; and I myself will raise him up on
the last day.[30]

Salvation, resurrection of the dead, ascent to the Father –
indeed, all aspects of mystic experience and true spiritual
life – cannot be learnt by "rote" or "book learning" or by
"professional skills". No amount of repetition of verbal
prayers, of theological speculation or intellectual knowledge
of the scriptures will lead to mystic experience. This
"heavenly thing" is entirely due to the "grace" of the Brother
or Saviour, and is the "gift" of the heavenly Father. And the
author reinforces his point by quoting John's gospel. Only
the soul that is drawn by the Father will be "raised up", and
will ascend to him.

The Repentance of the Soul

It is therefore fitting to pray to the Father and to call on him
with all our soul – not externally with the lips but with the
spirit, which is inward, which came forth from the Depth –
sighing; repenting for the life we lived; confessing our sins;
perceiving the empty deception we were in, and the empty
zeal; weeping over how we were in darkness and in the
waves (of the stormy sea); mourning for ourselves, that he
might have pity on us; hating ourselves for how we are now.
Again the Saviour said:

Blessed are those who mourn, for it is they who will be
pitied; blessed, those who are hungry, for it is they who
will be filled.[31]

As a consequence, he says, we must turn to the Father within
ourselves. External words have little meaning; it is the turning of our spirit to God which is important, as Jesus said.[32]
The "spirit, which is inward, which came forth from the
Depth" is the soul – the "Depth" being another expression

used for God as the unfathomable, unplumbable Source of all, from which the soul originates.[33]

We have to sincerely repent and turn away from the profligate "life we lived", he insists. We must become aware of the illusion and "empty deception" of the ephemeral world. We must realize that the mental and emotional "zeal" with which we may have approached life and religion are "empty", since they do not lead to salvation or even to a truly spiritual life. We must understand the nature of the "darkness" of this world and its stormy character, longing for release from the condition in which we find ourselves. The author then quotes Jesus, taking "those who mourn" to be those who repent and long for mercy, and "those who are hungry" to be those who hunger for true spiritual life. And he continues, citing a number of texts which emphasize the importance of repentance:

Again he (Jesus) said:

> If one does not hate his soul (life in this world),
>   he cannot follow me.[34]

For the beginning of salvation is repentance. Therefore:

> Before Christ's appearance came John,
>   preaching the baptism of repentance.[35]

And repentance takes place in distress and grief. But the Father is good and loves humanity, and he hears the soul that calls upon him and sends it the light of salvation. Therefore, he said through the Spirit to the prophet:

> Say to the children of my people, "[If your] sins extend [from earth to] heaven, and if they become [red] like scarlet and blacker than [sackcloth and (even) if (then)] you return to Me with all your soul and say to Me, 'My Father,' I will heed you as a holy people."[36]

Again another place (in *Isaiah*):

> Thus says the Lord, the holy one of Israel: "If you return
> and sigh, then you will be saved and will know where
> you were when you trusted in what is empty."[37]

Again he said in another place (in *Isaiah*):

> Jerusalem wept much, saying, "Have pity on me." he will
> have pity on the sound of your weeping. And when he
> saw, he heeded you. And the Lord will give you bread of
> affliction and water of oppression. From now on, those
> who deceive will not approach you again. Your eyes will
> see those who are deceiving you.[38]

In the Judaic world and later in Christianity, too, repentance
was held to be an essential prelude to spiritual renewal, and
was commonly depicted in the literature of the time as
preceding baptism and mystic experience or revelation. It
appears in both the Old and New Testaments, as well as other
religious writings of the period. Traditional descriptions of
repentant individuals generally include sighing, moaning,
weeping, dressing in sackcloth, pouring ashes over the head
and so on. Mystically, repentance is significant because it
represents the turning point of a soul towards God. From
being a harlot, the soul wishes once again to become pure. It
takes place at the nadir of the soul's existence. Without this
turning inward, salvation is impossible. Hence, the writer
says, "the beginning of salvation is repentance".

True repentance, however, as he also says, is not a matter
of lip service. Nor is it anything to do with wallowing in
self-pity or self-abasement. It is internal and spiritual, a
matter of contacting the Spirit within. It is more a longing
for God than a rejection of the world. Naturally, the
individual may feel abashed by the way he or she has been
living, but the way of the Spirit is always positive, moving
forward towards God, not looking backward in a welter of

self-reproach and living in the past. That, after all, is only another form of self-expression or egotism.

The mind is always active; but it can move in only two primary directions – inward or outward. Generally, it moves outward into the world. True repentance is when the mind turns inward, towards the soul or spirit, and – ultimately – to God. This is why, quoting *Isaiah,* he says that as a result of this spiritual repentance and turning of the mind away from the world and towards God, "Those who deceive will not approach you again. Your eyes will see those who are deceiving you." As a soul progresses spiritually, the hollowness of the transient world becomes increasingly apparent. The illusions and mirages that once deceived by their allurement are seen for what they are, and lose their charm.

> Therefore it is fitting to pray to God night and day, spreading out our hands towards him as do people sailing in the middle of the sea: they pray to God with all their heart without hypocrisy. For those who pray hypocritically deceive only themselves. Indeed, it is in order that he might know who is worthy of salvation that God examines the inward parts and searches the bottom of the heart. For no one is worthy of salvation who still loves the place of deception.

The sincerity and longing must come from deep within, just as it does among those who are fearful of imminent shipwreck. There is no room for hypocrisy or play-acting when death is close at hand. People are stripped to their bare essentials, with their real feelings and characters exposed. Someone who speaks fine words of repentance, but "still loves the place of deception" – this world – is neither ready to follow the path to salvation nor are they worthy of it.

The writer then goes on to quote Homer's epic tale, the *Odyssey,* to illustrate his point that it is only when a soul turns with full sincerity to God that help is forthcoming. The *Odyssey* relates the trials and tribulations encountered by Odysseus (Ulysses) during his journey home to Ithaca after the siege of Troy (as related in the *Iliad*). Renowned for his courage, resourcefulness, ingenuity and strength, the journey nevertheless takes Odysseus ten years, during the course of which he loses all his companions. And – rather oddly – when he finally reaches home, he is only recognized by his wife Penelope after killing all her suitors, who had presumed him dead.

A number of ancient writers, however, have observed that even this story should be understood as an allegory of the soul's journey homeward, and that many other Greek myths should – at least in part – be interpreted as mystical allegories, too.[39]

When the narrative opens, Odysseus, longing for his home and wife, is being detained on the island of Ogygia by the seductive sea nymph, Calypso, who has held him as her captive lover for seven years. The story would have been known to almost everyone in the Hellenized world of those times, and the writer only needed to recall the scene with a few words of paraphrase:

Therefore it is written in the poet:

Odysseus sat on the island weeping and grieving and turning his face from the words of Calypso and from her tricks, longing to see his village and smoke coming forth from it.[40]

And had he not [received] help from heaven, [he would] not [have been able to return] to his village.

In the story, the gods hold council and, seeing the home-sickness of Odysseus, they take pity on him and send a messenger to Calypso, instructing her to release him immediately. Later, Homer describes the scene as Calypso approaches to tell him he is free at last to leave:

His (Odysseus') eyes were wet with weeping as they always were. Life with its sweetness was ebbing away in the tears he had for his lost home. For the Nymph had long since ceased to please. At nights, it is true, he had to sleep with her in the vaulted cavern – cold lover, ardent lady. But the days found him sitting on the rocks or sands, torturing himself with tears, groans and heartache, and looking out with streaming eyes across the watery wilderness.

Homer, Odyssey 5:150–55, HO p.74

The same longing for home is also expressed in the *Odyssey*, when Helen is reminiscing of her time in Troy after deserting her husband Menelaus and running off with Paris (the incident which started the Trojan War). After some time, she realizes her mistake and begins to long for her home once more and for her "good, understanding, handsome husband" or – as another translation has it – her "husband who lacked nothing in intelligence and looks".[41] She realizes that she has been deceived by Aphrodite, the goddess of physical love:

Again, Helen, … saying:

"I had suffered a change of heart. I was longing to go home again."[42]

For she sighed, saying:

"It is Aphrodite who deceived me and brought me out of my village. My only daughter I left behind me, and my good, understanding, handsome husband."[43]

For when the soul leaves her perfect husband because of the treachery of Aphrodite, who exists here in the act of begetting, then she will suffer harm. But if she sighs and repents, she will be restored to her house.

Subsequently, Helen is rescued by the Greeks and their allies after a long and difficult war. Whether originally intended as an allegory or not, the writer of the present text draws on Homer to demonstrate that sincere repentance and longing for home is required before a response from the Divine is forthcoming.

To conclude his discussion, he then reverts to the *Exodus* allegory, where the "land of Egypt" is again the physical universe:

> Certainly Israel would not have been visited in the first place, to be brought out of the land of Egypt, out of the house of bondage, if it had not sighed to God and wept for the oppression of its labours. Again it is written in the *Psalms:*
>
> > I was greatly troubled in my groaning.
> > I will bathe my bed
> >   and my cover each night with my tears.
> > I have become old in the midst of all my enemies.
> > Depart from me, all you who work at lawlessness,
> >   for behold the Lord has heard the cry of my weeping,
> >   and the Lord has heard my prayer.[44]
>
> If we repent, truly God will heed us, he who is long-suffering and abundantly merciful, to whom is the glory for ever and ever. Amen.

This parable, then, with its accompanying discussion and citations from respected Jewish, Christian and Greek sources, tells the essential story of the soul. It speaks of her descent from God, her sad experiences in this world, and her return home with the help of a Saviour or Master. In the mystic literature, especially of early Christian times, this story is told and retold in many different guises, often emphasizing different aspects of the universal mystic path, but expressing the same essential spiritual truths, using the same recurring metaphors and themes.

NOTES AND REFERENCES

1. See *Appendix* for more details of this text.
2. For text, *cf. Expository Treatise on the Soul, NHS21* pp.144–69.
3. *E.g. John* 2:13–16; *Luke* 19:45–46; *Mark* 11:15–17; *Matthew* 21:12–13 (in *GJ* pp.205–8). See also *GJ* index: robbers.
4. See *e.g. GJ* index: animals; enemies; beasts, wild *or* savage; *The Lost Sheep and the Prodigal Son*, in *PSW* p.14; *The Pearl Merchant* in *PSW* pp.59–60, 66–67, 69; *The Radiant Birds on the Tree of Life*, in *PSW* p.144.
5. *Cf.* Rumi, *Masnavi* II:2131, *MJR2* p.331.
6. *Jeremiah* 3:1–4 *(LXX)*.
7. *Hosea* 2:4–9 *(LXX)*, 2:2–7 *(MT)*.
8. *Hosea* 2:2, *JB*.
9. *E.g.* in OT: *Deuteronomy* 4:24; *Isaiah* 1:21–26; *Jeremiah* 2:2, 3:1, 6:12; *Ezekiel* 16:1–63, 23:1–49. *Cf.* also *Isaiah* 50:1, 54:6–7, 62:4–5; *Psalms* 45; *Song of Songs.*
10. *Ezekiel* 16:23–26 *(LXX)*.
11. *Cf. Acts* 15:20, 29, 21:25; *1 Thessalonians* 4:3; *1 Corinthians* 6:18; *2 Corinthians* 7:1.
12. *1 Corinthians* 5:9–10.
13. *Ephesians* 6:12 (in *GJ* pp.495–96, 752).
14. See *e.g. Trimorphic Protennoia* 49 (in *GJ* p.761); *Pistis Sophia* 100, 111–13, 147 (in *GJ* pp.434–36, 442, 493).
15. See *e.g. GJ* index: Brother; First-born; Bridegroom.
16. **Door:** *Book of Revelation* 3:8, 20, 4:1 (in *GJ* pp.414, 748); *John* 10:2ff. (in *GJ* pp.302, 749); *Matthew* 7:7–8 (in *GJ* pp.746–47). See also *GJ* index: door.
    Strait gate, narrow way: *Matthew* 7:13–14 (in *GJ* pp.743–44). See also *GJ* index: gates.
    Eye of a needle: *Matthew* 19:24ff. (in *GJ* pp.744–45).
17. See "Introduction", pp.7–8, *The Bridegroom*, pp.25–33; see also *e.g. GJ* pp.843–50.
18. See *The Damsel of Light*, pp.64–65. See also *The Good Samaritan*, in *PSW* p.19; *The Raising of Lazarus*, in *PSW* p.53; *The Palace of King Gundaphorus*, in *PSW* p.120; *The Radiant Birds on the Tree of Life*, in *PSW* p.145; *Adam Gets a Letter*, in *PSW* p.178. See also *e.g. GJ* index: fragrance.
19. *John* 10:30, 14:9–11 (in *GJ* pp.515–16).
20. *Genesis* 2:24 *(LXX)*.
21. *Cf. Genesis* 3:16; *1 Corinthians* 11:3; *Ephesians* 5:23.
22. *Psalms* 44:11–12 *(LXX)*, 45:10–11 *(MT)*.
23. *Genesis* 12:1 *(LXX)*.
24. *Matthew* 13:3–9, 18–23 (in *GJ* pp.720–23). See also *GJ* index: Seed.

25. *John* 3:3–8 (in *GJ* pp.677–78). See also *GJ* index: born again; born of the Spirit.
26. See *GJ* pp.806–18.
27. *Cf. Mark* 10:43–45. See also *GJ* pp.489–96.
28. See *e.g. GJ* pp.806–18.
29. *Psalms* 102:1–5 *(LXX)*, 103:1–5 *(MT)*.
30. *John* 6:44 (in *GJ* pp.530, 678–89).
31. *Cf. Matthew* 5:4, 6 (in *GJ* pp.833–34); *Luke* 6:21.
32. *John* 4:23–24 (in *GJ* pp.288–90).
33. *E.g. Authoritative Teaching* 32, *NHS11* pp.280–81; *Manichaean Psalm Book, MPB* p.133.
34. *Cf. Luke* 14:26, *Matthew* 16:25.
35. *Cf. Mark* 1:4, 15; *Matthew* 3:2, 11, 4:17; *Luke* 3:3; *Acts* 13:24.
36. *Cf. 1 Clement* 8:3 (in *e.g. WAF* p.12).
37. *Isaiah* 30:15 *(LXX)*.
38. *Isaiah* 30:19–20 *(LXX)*.
39. See *e.g.* Eustathius (in *SBEG* p.191); Hippolytus on the Naasenes, *Refutation of All Heresies* V:II-III (in *e.g. RAH* p.135*ff.*); *cf. Clementine Homilies* IV:24 (in *e.g. CH* p.100); Hippolytus, *Refutation of All Heresies* V:XV, VI:XIV (in *e.g. RAH* pp.176–79, 210–12); Plato, *Republic* II:378–79 (in *e.g. DP2* p.30). See also Numenius of Apamea, Cronius and Porphyry (in *e.g. SBEG* pp.191–92).
40. Homer, *Odyssey* 1:48–59, 4:558.
41. Homer, *Odyssey* 4:264, *HO* p.52.
42. Homer, *Odyssey* 4:260–61; *cf. HO* p.52.
43. Homer, *Odyssey* 4:261–64; *cf.* HO p.52.
44. *Psalms* 6:7–10 *(LXX)*, 6:6–9 *(MT)*.

FOUR

The Damsel of Light

There is clearly something very special about the soul incarnate in a human form, for the topic crops up constantly in mystic literature. Half-beast, half-angel, with the capacity to become worse than one or better than the other, mystics seem to give humanity a far better press than, on the face of it, we deserve. It all seems to stem from our inherent potential to realize God within ourselves, something which a dog, a cat or a chimpanzee, however intelligent, affectionate and good-natured they may be, can never do.

The subject is addressed in an allegorical anecdote encountered at the beginning of the *Acts of Thomas*, where the apostle, *en route* to India in the company of Abbanes the merchant, finds himself at a marriage party. As a starting point for his book, the author knows exactly what he is doing, for he begins with the spiritual potential of a human being. He opens his story with an echo of Jesus' parable of the wedding feast, where all souls are invited to the mystic marriage:

> And the king … sent heralds to proclaim everywhere that all should come to the marriage, rich and poor, bond and free, strangers and citizens. And if any refuse, and come not to the marriage, he shall answer for it to the king.
>
> *Acts of Thomas 4, ANT p.366*

The story then progresses until a flute girl joins the party and, discovering Judas Thomas,

stood over him and played at his head for a long space. Now
this flute girl was by race an Hebrew.

Acts of Thomas 5, ANT p.367

The "flute girl" is "an Hebrew", a fellow countryman of the
apostle. She is his associate or fellow traveller on the mystic
path. Her playing of the flute – whose haunting tones are
commonly used to describe the divine Music of the higher
realms – is probably a further hint to her symbolic and
mystical significance. The flute is specifically stated to be
"played at his head", implying that the entire creation lies
within man, and that the starting point for this discovery
lies in the head, at the eye centre or single eye.

Judas Thomas underlines this interpretation when he
breaks into a song, where it becomes clear that the flute girl,
the "damsel", is symbolic of the soul incarnate in a human
form. He also describes her in ways that are reminiscent of
parts of the biblical *Song of Songs* where the lover and
Beloved recount each other's mystic beauty. So perhaps the
author drew his inspiration for this passage from the *Song of
Songs*. The symbolism is expressly mystical:

> The damsel is the daughter of light,
> > in whom consists and dwells
> > the proud brightness of kings.
> And the sight of her is delightful:
> > she shines with beauty and cheer.
>
> Her garments are like the flowers of spring,
> > and from them a waft of Fragrance is borne;
> And in the crown of her head the King is established,
> > who with his immortal Food (ambrosia)
> > nourishes them that are founded upon him.

Acts of Thomas 6; cf. ANT p.367

The "damsel" is the soul, a drop of the light of the Lord, the
mystic King. She is beautiful, radiant and joyous. Her

natural "garments" or robe are full of life and the vibrancy of springtime, imbued with the "Fragrance" of the Breath of Life, the Creative Word. The mystic "King" lies within her head, "at the crown", the highest point in the human form, from where he feeds the souls of "them that are founded upon him" – his initiates – with the "immortal Food" of the Word.

> And in her head is set Truth,
> and with her feet she shows forth joy.
> *Acts of Thomas 6; cf. ANT p.367*

A double meaning is intended. Many Eastern mystics have said, in one way or another, that the spiritual journey begins at the soles of the feet and ends at the crown of the head. The Lord is at the "head" or Source of the creation while the human form lies at the "foot", in the physical universe. For the physically incarnate soul, God is her "head" or Source. He is the "Truth" of her existence. "Her feet" refers to the human form where she can learn to dance with "joy". Her spiritual journey thus begins with "joy" in the human form, and culminates in union with God, with the "Truth". This is the first meaning.

The human form, however, is also a microcosm of the entire creation, and a humanly incarnate soul begins the spiritual journey by withdrawing all the attention and consciousness from the body. Beginning from the feet, the currents of the mind and soul are withdrawn to the single eye and go yet higher within, finally reaching God. The journey starts at the "feet" and ends in the "head". Consequently, the "damsel" – the soul in human form – "shows forth joy". As she progresses on the mystic path, she dances inwardly with great joy.

> And her mouth is opened, and it becomes her well:
> thirty and two are they that sing praises to her.
> *Acts of Thomas 6; cf. ANT p.367*

"Her mouth is opened" signifies the soul's openness to the flow of divine grace, and "it becomes her well" – she is made beautiful by it. "Thirty-two are they that sing praises to her" are the thirty-two teeth in the mouth, representing all that lies within her. Every 'part' of the soul is full of joy and bliss to be receiving this grace.

> Her tongue is like the curtain of the door
> > that waves to and fro
> > for them that enter in.
> Her neck is set in the fashion of steps
> > that the First Maker has wrought.
> And her two hands signify and show,
> > proclaiming the dance of the happy ages,
> > and her fingers point out the gates of the city.
>
> *Acts of Thomas 6; cf. ANT p.367*

"Her tongue" controls access to what lies within, to that which flows into "her mouth". It represents the "door", the single eye, through which the soul may "enter in", and discover the Living Waters which flow into her inner "well". The tongue is a major organ through which the mind expresses itself, and until the mind's desire for outward expression is brought under control, the soul and mind can never go within.

The tongue as a flapping curtain "that waves to and fro" symbolizes the mind's habit of continually repeating thoughts. Thoughts of the world shut the "door" to the inner realms. Thoughts of what lies beyond the "door" enable the mind to concentrate at the inner "door". Then the "door" will open, and the mind and soul will "enter in".

The mind is never still, and the soul goes wherever the thoughts and desires of the mind lead it. If thoughts are of the world, then the mind and soul stay in the world. But if, through spiritual practice, the thoughts of the outer world are replaced by thoughts of the inner worlds, then the mind and soul will slowly make their way through the inner "door" or single eye and "enter" those higher realms. This is accomplished by careful and concentrated repetition of particular names which have an association only with the inner journey. With the mind focused in repetition of these names, the attention slowly withdraws from the outer world and enters the world within.

But it is a slow and gradual process. Spiritual practice is a struggle because the mind continually "waves to and fro", and does not permit the mind and soul to "enter in".

"Her neck is set in the fashion of steps" because the soul and the mind have to rise up from the lower part of the body to the head, through the narrow passage of the neck, as if by a ladder.

The "two hands ... proclaiming the dance of the happy ages" depict the dance of duality, of good and bad, and all the pairs of opposites that comprise this world, in which the soul is entangled and which continues age after age.

The ten "fingers pointing out the gates of the city" refer to the ten gates or openings to the city of the body. They are like indicators, pointers or signs to the esoteric constitution of the human form. Of these ten apertures, nine open into the world and one – the tenth gate or single eye – opens inwards, leading to the inner realms. The nine openings, described as such in the *Upanishads*[1] and other mystic literature of India,[2] are the two eyes, the two ears, the two nostrils, the mouth and the two lower openings. The attention of the mind and soul has its headquarters at the single eye. From here it spreads into the world through these nine openings. But, at the tenth gate, it can focus and go inside. These "gates of the city" and the "tenth gate" are also referred to in the gnostic allegory, *The Pearl Merchant*.[3]

The song of the "damsel" continues:

> Her (inner) chamber is bright with light,
>> and breathes forth the fragrance of balsam and all spices,
>> and gives off a sweet smell of myrrh and Indian leaf.

> And within are myrtles strewn on the floor,
>> and garlands of all manner of scented flowers,
>> and the door posts (?) are adorned with reeds (?).
> And surrounding her, her groomsmen keep her,
>> the number of whom is seven,
>> whom she herself has chosen.
> And her bridesmaids are seven, and they dance before her.
> And twelve in number are they that serve before her
>> and are subject unto her,
>> which have their aim and their look
>> towards the Bridegroom,
>> that by the sight of him they may be enlightened.
>
> *Acts of Thomas 6–7; cf. ANT p.367*

The poet is now describing the soul's inner being – "her chamber". It is "bright with light" and gives off a "fragrance" of healing herbs and spices, and the perfume "of all manner of scented flowers". The soul is inwardly inundated with light and with the fragrance or essence of divine Music.

The "door posts", the supporting pillars of her chamber, "are adorned with reeds" – evocative of the Sound of the reed flute, heard in the high spiritual region that lies on the threshold of eternity. This realm, so close to God, is full with the sweet pain of separation from and the longing for union with him. It is this love and longing that supports and gives life to the soul's inner chamber of being.

The seven "groomsmen" and the seven "bridesmaids" dancing before her are the seven heavens with their seven rulers, in the ancient Middle Eastern description of the creation. They "dance" before the soul as her playmates and companions when she has risen above them and looks down from the state of a true bride, as a soul unified with the Lord. The metaphor is similar to that of the seven virgins who accompany Aseneth in the story of *Joseph and Aseneth,* and who are described as the "seven pillars in the City of Refuge".[4]

The "twelve" who "serve before her" are the twelve

primary *aeons* (powers) of gnostic terminology who emanate from God as aspects of the Creative Word, forming and administering the creation.[5] They have "their aim and their look towards the Bridegroom, that by the sight of him they may be enlightened." That is, they derive their power and light from the divine Bridegroom, the Word.

> And forever shall they be with her in that eternal joy;
> And shall be at that marriage
>   at which the princes are gathered together;
> And shall attend that banquet
>   of which the eternal ones are accounted worthy;
> And shall put on royal raiment and be clad in bright robes.
>
> *Acts of Thomas 7; cf. ANT p.367*

At the supreme "marriage" of union with the Lord, the soul dances the primal dance that moves and sustains all creation, the supreme dance of divine love. All the "princes" or Masters are present, attending the spiritual banquet at which the "eternal ones", the pure souls who have attained salvation "are accounted worthy". They are "worthy" because they are wearing their wedding garments, their "bright robes" of glory, signifying the inherent royalty and pristine spirituality of the soul.

> And in joy and exultation shall they both be,
>   and shall glorify the Father of All,
>   whose proud light they have received,
>   and are enlightened by the sight of their Lord;
> Whose immortal Food they have received,
>   which has no impurity;
> And have drunk of the wine,
>   which gives them neither thirst nor desire.
> And they have glorified and praised
>   with the Living Spirit,
>   the Father of Truth and the Mother of Wisdom.
>
> *Acts of Thomas 7; cf. ANT pp.367–68*

The soul with her Master, the mystic bride and Bridegroom, worship with the natural love and reverence of such a high spiritual estate. They are fed by the "immortal Food" and "wine" of the divine Music which quenches all desire and thirst for anything other than God. They are exalted and illuminated by the "Living Spirit" of the Lord, the great "Father of Truth" and the "Mother of Wisdom". They are one with the Lord and his creative Power, the Mother of all created things.

NOTES AND REFERENCES

1.   *E.g. Shvetashvatara Upanishad* III:18; *Katha Upanishad* II:2.1; *Bhagavad Gita* V:13.
2.   There are a great many such references from different mystics, as in the *Adi Granth, e.g.* Guru Ramdas, *Adi Granth* p.1323.
3.   See *The Pearl Merchant,* in *PSW* pp.60, 68.
4.   See *Joseph and Aseneth,* p.152.
5.   *E.g.* **Nag Hammadi codices:** *Apocryphon of John* 8; *Eugnostos the Blessed* 84; *First Apocalypse of James* 26; *Gospel of the Egyptians* 57–58; *Sophia of Jesus Christ* 106–7. *Bruce Codex: First Book of Jeu* (throughout); *Second Book of Jeu* 49–52; *Pistis Sophia* 7, 10, 14–15, 27–28, 30–31, 46, 50, 57, 66, 67, 76, 84, 136, 138; *Untitled Text* (throughout).

   Manichaean texts: *Manichaean Psalm Book* CCXIX, CCXXIII, *MPB* pp.1, 9, 144; *Psalms of Heracleides, Manichaean Psalm Book, MPB* p.198.

FIVE

Joseph and Aseneth

The Story of Joseph

The story is related in *Genesis* of how Joseph – the favoured son of Jacob (son of Isaac, son of Abraham, of the lineage of Shem, son of Noah, descendant of Adam) – is sold as a slave to the nomadic Ishmaelites by his eleven jealous brothers. He is subsequently carried off to Egypt, where he is bought by Potiphar, captain of the guard, and taken into his household. There, fortune smiles upon him, at least for a while. As a consequence of his noble bearing, his honest disposition and because the "Lord was with Joseph", he soon rises to the position of overseer of Potiphar's house and estate, the Egyptian captain entrusting to him all matters concerning the administration of his property. Says *Genesis:*

And the Lord was with Joseph, and he became a prosperous man; and he was in the house of his master, the Egyptian. And his master saw that the Lord was with him, and that the Lord made all that he did to prosper in his hand. And Joseph found favour in his sight, and he served him. And he made him overseer over his house, and put him in charge of all that he had.

And it came to pass from the time that he had made him overseer in his house, and over all that he had, that the Lord blessed the Egyptian's house for Joseph's sake; and the blessing of the Lord was upon all that he had in the house, and in the field. And he left all that he had in Joseph's charge; and he knew not what he possessed, save the bread that he ate. And Joseph was handsome and good-looking.

Genesis 39:2–6; cf. KJV, RSV

Now Joseph is a handsome young man and Potiphar's wife takes a fancy to him. Joseph, however, as a virtuous man of God, rejects her advances. Stung by his rejection, she claims that Joseph has tried to take advantage of her. As a result, Potiphar, believing his wife, has Joseph thrown into prison. But, repeats *Genesis,* the "Lord was with Joseph"[1] and, even in captivity, he is soon given a position of trust, as overseer of the other prisoners.

In his earlier life, living with his father, his mother and his eleven brothers in Canaan, Joseph had had two dreams of a symbolic nature, foretelling that his parents and brothers would one day bow down to him.[2] In prison, he finds that he is able to accurately interpret the dreams of others. In the ancient world, dreaming and a skill in dream interpretation were both considered indications of divine favour. Dream interpreters were among the personnel of many pagan temples.[3] Also, in sacred writings, dreams of a revelational nature were often used as veiled references to inner or mystic experience, since dreams and spiritual practice are commonly nocturnal, both entailing temporary unconsciousness of the physical world.[4]

Joseph gains his reputation by accurately interpreting the dreams of two fellow inmates – Pharaoh's butler and chief baker. He foretells that the butler will soon be released, while the baker will be hanged.[5] This happens as predicted and some two years later, after Pharaoh himself has experienced a vivid and notable dream, the butler remembers Joseph, advising his master of Joseph's interpretative ability.

Pharaoh calls for Joseph, who interprets the dream to mean that there will be seven years of ample harvest followed by seven years of famine.[6] Joseph therefore advises

Pharaoh to gather a vast store of food during the seven years of plenty in order to see them through the seven years of famine. Little could be worse than famine and crop failure in the ancient world, or indeed at any time, and advance notice was naturally of inestimable value, especially to a ruler who wished to govern well and remain in favour with his people. Therefore, trusting Joseph's interpretation and being greatly pleased with him, Pharaoh has Joseph released from prison, making him a ruler in Egypt, second only to himself. Joseph's primary mandate is to collect grain during the seven years of plenty and to administer its distribution during the subsequent years of famine. And, as before, *Genesis* emphasizes Joseph's godliness:

> And Pharaoh said to his servants, "Where else can we find someone such as this, a man in whom dwells the Spirit of God?" And Pharaoh said to Joseph, "Since God has showed you all this, and there is none so discreet and wise as you, you shall be overseer in my house, and according to your word shall all my people be ruled. Only in the throne will I be greater than you."
>
> *Genesis 41:38–40; cf. KJV*

Then, in a traditional gesture of trust, Pharaoh gives Joseph his own signet ring, his seal of authority. He also dresses him in "fine linen", puts "a gold chain about his neck", and gives him his "second chariot" as his means of transport.[7] And to complete his favours, he arranges for Joseph, now aged thirty, to be married:

> And Pharaoh … gave him to wife, Aseneth, the daughter of Potipherah (Gk. *Pentephres*), priest of On (Gk. *Heliopolis*). And Joseph went out over all the land of Egypt. And Joseph was thirty years old when he stood before Pharaoh, king of Egypt.
>
> *Genesis 41:46, KJV*

According to two further comments in *Genesis,* two children
– Manasseh and Ephraim – are subsequently born to the
couple.[8] It is upon these three brief mentions of Aseneth
that the legend of *Joseph and Aseneth* has been embellished
and woven, set within the general context of the biblical
story of Joseph.

The Text [9]

Joseph and Aseneth, as this story is commonly called, comes
from the early Christian period. Almost certainly written in
Greek, there is no evidence of any earlier tradition of it as an
orally transmitted legend. The details of the story were thus
composed by a particular writer at a particular time, rather
than evolving out of folklore, although no author's name is
associated with it.

The essential theme is the betrothal and marriage of
Joseph – portrayed as a man of the Spirit and a Son of God
– to Aseneth, daughter of Pentephres, priest of Heliopolis.
The meaning of the story, however, is clearly symbolic,
containing many elements that convey a primarily gnostic
message.

There is early evidence of this. The earliest known manuscript of the story is a Syriac translation, dated no later than
569 AD, where it is preceded by a letter addressed to a
certain Moses of Ingila. The writer of the letter says that he
found the text in a very old Greek book, and asks for a
translation and interpretation of the story, which he clearly
regards as an allegory. Only a part of Moses' answer is
preserved, but from this it seems that Moses of Ingila understood the text to describe the union of the soul (symbolized as
Aseneth) with the divine *Logos* or Word of God (represented
by Joseph).[10]

Although the story is entertaining, whoever wrote *Joseph
and Aseneth* was not a purist in the use of allegory. There is
little subtlety in the choice of metaphors. There is also much

in the story which does not readily lend itself to allegorical interpretation, and which must be taken as simple narrative alone. The writer also provides detailed descriptions which might be expected to possess a symbolic meaning, like the elaborate account of the garments and ornaments worn by Aseneth. But unless the text, as we now have it, has seen considerable corruption since originally penned, it is likely that these descriptions were only intended in a general sense, and were simply conforming to a literary tradition of ornate narrative. It is also possible, of course, that the symbolic meaning of such passages may be obscure nowadays because it relates to local cultural and religious beliefs and practices of which we are now unaware.

Another possibility is that the writer was using motifs and metaphors, common to other allegories and writings of his time, but without possessing a clear-cut understanding of their meaning or of how they might be fully used in an allegorical setting. Such passages were thus used for their colourful narrative effect rather than the conveying of a particular, codified meaning. In other passages, however, the spiritual meaning is stated explicitly with very little use of metaphor, as in the psalms or prayers of Aseneth. The writer also has a habit of explaining his imagery to ensure that his message has been understood. This may not be the sign of a master craftsman at work, but the story is enjoyable nonetheless. It also makes the interpretation easier.

Probably written sometime in the first century, *Joseph and Aseneth* exhibits a rich blend of Jewish, Christian and Greek influences. It has been suggested that the story as we have it is a Christian overwriting of an earlier Jewish text. The essential themes, however, are gnostic, and the writer himself was probably someone of Jewish and Christian background who saw spiritual truths in all the religious traditions of the times.

Understood in this way, the meaning of *Joseph and Aseneth* – as observed by Moses of Ingila more than a millennium ago – is essentially that of the soul coming into contact with the Word or *Logos* personified as the gnostic Saviour or Master. The fall of Wisdom (Gk. *Sophia*, Heb. *Hokhmah*) into the realm of darkness (this world) and her eventual rescue by the *Logos* in the form of a Saviour is a fundamental and recurrent story underlying gnostic belief in the early Christian period.

The 'conversion' experience of Aseneth, therefore, is actually that of the soul touched by the divine grace of the Saviour. It is neither specifically Jewish nor Christian in character, but represents an experience which transcends both. Likewise, the eventual marriage of Aseneth to Joseph symbolizes the inner union of the soul with the *Logos*, following mystic baptism or initiation. This baptism is an inner affair that is probably the origin of the ritual baptisms of Christianity and some ancient Jewish sects. Other aspects of the story, such as the appearance of an all-knowing "man of light" in the form and likeness of Joseph, and who seems privy to the counsels of God, are immediately and more readily understood from a gnostic angle than from a Jewish or Christian point of view.

The text as we now have it has undoubtedly suffered from some tinkering at the hands of Christian editors. Editorial tampering is also apparent when the various extant translations – the Latin, Armenian, Syriac, Slavonic and so on – are compared. Nonetheless, the essential text does not appear to have been too severely distorted.

The story of *Joseph and Aseneth* falls naturally into two parts: firstly, the meeting and marriage of Joseph and Aseneth and, secondly, their later life. Based upon an analysis of the text, some scholars have suggested that the second part is the addition of a later author. There is significant evidence for this. The first part, for example, makes frequent and consistent use of spiritual metaphors, the second does not. At least, it would require considerable intellectual contortions to interpret it as an allegory or even as possessing any particular spiritual or mystic meaning. As regards the present exposition, therefore, it has been omitted. Otherwise, nothing that could have belonged to the original text has been excluded.

Whether or not *Joseph and Aseneth* was once considered a Jewish or a gnostic text, its history shows it to have been adopted into mainstream Christianity from at least the fourth or fifth centuries onward. Its appeal, no doubt, was its inspirational character as well as everyone's love of a good story. In many instances, it would have been read aloud at small gatherings. Its gnostic symbolism could have been understood as reflecting Christian eucharistic and baptismal ritual, and would have caused no difficulties. Some of its doctrinal aspects, however, such as the pre-existence and immortality of the soul are more Greek and gnostic in character than orthodox Christian. But despite these features, it seems to have survived more or less intact. The average Christian reader was probably more interested in the story than in a detailed analysis of its doctrinal implications.

Joseph and Aseneth may be little known at the present time, but that has not always been the case. Although few traces of the story remain from before the tenth and eleventh centuries, from then onward, for about six or seven centuries, the story gained in popularity. In the beginning, this was probably due to two Latin translations made around the year 1200. Subsequently, in the mid-thirteenth century, a certain Vincent de Beauvais (*c.*1190–1264) produced a condensed version of one of the two Latin translations in his *Speculum Historiale,* a supposed history of the world from the creation down to 1244–53 AD. His version of *Joseph and Aseneth* was later reproduced as an independent text, both printed and hand-copied, and was translated into many European languages, including (in the words of C. Burchard):

Czech, Dutch, English, French, German, Polish, Russian, and Scandinavian, including Icelandic, down to the eighteenth century. In the sixteenth century, *Joseph and Aseneth*, Part I, was made into a play for Corpus Christi Day.

C. Burchard, OTP2 p.198

Burchard then completes the brief history, up to the present day:

> In 1670, Philipp von Zesen, the renowned German baroque writer, had his most important novel, *Assenat*, probably the first one on this subject, printed in Amsterdam. He used a Dutch version of Vincent's abridgement as one of his sources. Large portions have gone into his text, others are quoted verbatim in the learned footnotes appended to the novel according to the custom of the time. Of the thirty engravings which adorn the volume, several illustrate scenes stemming from *Joseph and Aseneth....*
>
> After this period, the European reading public gradually lost interest in *Joseph and Aseneth*. Nineteenth-century scholarship rediscovered it and most of its versions; and owing to two short notes by G.D. Kilpatrick and J. Jeremias in 1952, it has been viewed with growing interest by students of early Judaism and Christianity.
>
> *C. Burchard, OTP2 pp.198–99*

This, then, is some of the background to the story of *Joseph and Aseneth.*

I. THE HOUSE OF PENTEPHRES

Pentephres had a Virgin Daughter

The narrative begins soon after the appointment of Joseph as Pharaoh's chief minister:

> It came to pass in the first year of the seven years of plenty, in the second month, on the fifth of the month, that Pharaoh sent Joseph to make a tour throughout the entire land of Egypt. And in the fourth month of the first year, on the

eighteenth of the month, Joseph came to the district of
Heliopolis. And he gathered corn in that land, as plentiful
as the sand on the seashore.

Now there was a certain man in that city, a satrap of
Pharaoh, the chief of all Pharaoh's satraps and noblemen.
He was very rich and wise and gentle; and because his
wisdom exceeded that of all Pharaoh's noblemen, he was
also one of Pharaoh's counsellors. And his name was
Pentephres, a priest of Heliopolis.

And Pentephres had a virgin daughter of about eighteen
years of age, tall and graceful, more beautiful to look upon
than any other virgin on the earth. She was quite unlike the
daughters of the Egyptians, but in every respect resembled
the daughters of the Hebrews. She was as tall as Sarah, as
fair as Rebecca, and as beautiful as Rachel; and this virgin's
name was Aseneth. And the fame of her beauty spread
throughout that land, even to the ends of the world, so that
all the sons of the noblemen and satraps and kings sought
her hand in marriage, all of them young and valiant. And
there was jealousy and rivalry between them on account of
Aseneth, and they began to fight among themselves because
of her.

And Pharaoh's first-born son heard about her, and he
continuously entreated his father to give her to him as his
wife, saying, "Father, give me Aseneth the daughter of
Pentephres the priest of Heliopolis for my wife."

But Pharaoh his father said to him, "Why do you seek a
wife who is beneath you? One day you will be king of all
this land. No! Behold, the daughter of Joakim, the king of
Moab, is betrothed to you. She is a queen and very beautiful
indeed: take her as your wife."

Drawing on the brief citations in *Genesis*, the main characters of the drama are introduced. Pentephres is identified as
a priest of Heliopolis, Aseneth as his daughter, and Joseph as
the first ruler of Egypt after Pharaoh. In a true allegory,
every detail of this description would have a particular

meaning. The "first year", the "seven years of plenty", "gathering corn as the sand of the sea", Pharaoh, Joseph, the city of Heliopolis,[11] Aseneth as a virgin, her age, the details of her appearance and so on would all possess a symbolic meaning. But it is unlikely that anything of such a detailed and specific nature is intended here.

As it stands, the harvest season in which Aseneth meets Joseph may have a symbolic significance, but even this is not clearly indicated. Perhaps it signifies the fruition of God's original creative intent – for the soul to realize her divine heritage and reap the harvest of true spirituality through divine union or marriage with the *Logos*. But the spelling out of the exact year, month and day is a traditional introduction to ancient writings, equivalent to an extended "once upon a time", and it is doubtful whether it embodies any particular meaning.

Aseneth, as we have said, represents the soul. She is portrayed as youthful, beautiful, pure and desirable, symbolizing the intrinsic nature of the soul as life-giving, and full of a pristine and blissful loveliness. She is a virgin, a common feature of ancient romances, and the fact that she is eighteen means that she has been fending off suitors for some years.

She is also described as resembling the "daughters of the Hebrews", quite unlike the "daughters of the Egyptians". Possibly this comparison reflects the bias or prejudice of the writer. Even so, to the gnostics, Egypt – the place of slavery according to the traditional *Exodus* story – represents this world. Ancient Egypt was also perceived as a land of many gods and idol worship, the antithesis of the Jewish, Christian and mystic belief in one supreme Lord. The land of the Hebrews, on the other hand, signified the promised holy land, the eternal realm.

Consequently, for Aseneth – although Egyptian by birth – to be described as resembling a "daughter of the Hebrews" and unlike a "daughter of the Egyptians" depicts the soul's essential divinity, possessing none of the characteristics of this world. That Aseneth was actually born as an Egyptian suggests that although the soul is born into a physical body, she actually comes from a different realm altogether from that of the physical body in which she finds herself.

Aseneth's Penthouse Suite

Now Aseneth herself disdained and despised all men, being boastful and arrogant. Yet no man had ever seen her, for Pentephres had a tower adjoining his house, large and very high. And the top floor of this tower had ten chambers to it.

The first chamber was spacious and very lovely, adorned with beautiful marbles and draped with purple. Its walls glittered with precious and multicoloured stones, and the ceiling was of gold. Within it, the innumerable gods of the Egyptians were placed, in gold and silver. And Aseneth worshipped and feared them, and offered sacrifices to them daily.

In the second chamber were the treasure chests containing Aseneths's ornaments of gold and silver, in great quantity, rare and precious stones of great price, garments woven with gold, and fine and costly linen, and all the adornments of her maidenhood.

The third chamber was Aseneth's storeroom, containing all the good things of the earth (*i.e.* foodstuffs).

Seven virgins occupied the remaining seven chambers, one each. They waited on Aseneth, and were of the same age as she, all having been born on the same night. And she loved them greatly, and they were very beautiful, like the stars of heaven, and no man ever conversed with them, not even a boy.

Here, Aseneth symbolizes the soul in human form, isolated from the Divine and from all other souls by the illusion of egotism. She is "boastful and arrogant". We may not realise it, but egotism – the sense of individual self – is the heart of human existence as it is normally lived. We think of everything in relationship to 'me' – my home, my friends, my family, my money, my property, my job, my ideas and so on. Yet our sense of self is actually only an attribute or faculty of the mind for living life on this plane. It is not the true essence or reality of our being, even though, for the most part, we take it as the whole of our being and identity.

In the story, though said to be "boastful and arrogant", Aseneth does not actually behave that way. She is affectionate to her parents, servants and companions, and even her refusal to accept any of her suitors could be construed as only wanting the best for herself. Nevertheless, all human beings, however kind and warm-hearted, are still stalked by the demon of selfhood or egotism, and Aseneth is portrayed no differently.

That "no man had ever seen" Aseneth indicates that the soul is not visible to human eyes. As a result, almost no one is aware of the presence of the soul that lives within the human form as the source of their life and existence.

Pentephres' house with a "tower" was probably a palatial bungalow or a single-storey mansion with an upper floor built on at one end. This 'annexe', however, is substantial. Its upper floor has ten chambers, three containing Aseneth's possessions, the other seven being occupied by her seven lifelong companions, also as pure as she. This kind of detail suggests an allegorical significance.

The "tower" probably symbolizes the human form as a microcosm of creation. The soul 'lives' or has its centre 'at the top', in the head. But in the case of the soul overcome by egotism, the head is full of gods and idols. The soul does not know how to worship God, and instead 'worships' the idols or gods of worldliness, offering "sacrifices to them daily". Everything is continually sacrificed to the overpowering 'gods' of worldly entanglement of all kinds.

The ten chambers probably represent the regions of creation. The first three would be aspects of the eternal realm, the source of the soul's sustenance. The first chamber, where Aseneth lives, is beautiful and "very lovely" – but filled with idols, indicating that the soul does not appreciate her own natural and spiritual home.

The second chamber contains her fine clothes and ornaments. As traditional symbols of wealth, they signify both the garments of wealthy ostentation and worldliness as well as the pristine garment and spiritual 'ornamentation' of the soul, her 'robe of glory'. Later in the story, Aseneth fetches her ancient 'wedding garment' from this room. These are common motifs in the ancient mystic literature of the Middle East, as we have seen.[12] Incidentally, in ancient times, garments seem to have been folded and kept in chests, rather than being hung up in wardrobes.

The third chamber, the "storeroom" or larder, represents the sustenance of this world as well as that given to the soul from the eternal realm of pure Spirit. Later on, Aseneth gets food from this room which turns out to be of a spiritual nature.

The other seven chambers, occupied by the seven virgins, would be the seven heavens – an ancient belief of Judaism and Christianity and the Middle East in general. That the seven virgins were all "born on the same night" means that they were created at the same time as Aseneth, the soul. And no impure human being has "ever conversed with them", for impurity prevents the soul from leaving the body and ascending into the heavenly realms, where these pure souls dwell. Similar imagery is found in the allegory of the *Damsel of Light*, where the damsel or soul has seven bridesmaids and seven groomsmen.[13]

Now, Aseneth's large chamber, where she passed her time,[14] had three windows. The first was very large, and looked out eastward over the garden;[15] the second looked to the south; and the third to the north, onto the street where people passed by. And a golden bedstead stood in the chamber, facing east, decked with fine linen and a coverlet of purple woven with gold, embroidered with hyacinth, purple and white. In this bed, Aseneth slept by herself, and no man or woman ever sat upon it, except Aseneth alone.

Surrounding the house, there was a large garden enclosed by a very high wall, built of huge rectangular stones. And this garden had four gates, overlaid with iron, with eighteen strong young men-at-arms guarding each of them. And along the wall inside the garden, every kind of beautiful fruit-bearing tree had been planted, their fruit being ripe, for it was harvest time. And on the right of the garden, there was an ever bubbling spring of (*var.* living) water, and beneath the spring a great cistern that received the water from the spring, and out of which a river flowed through the middle of the garden, watering all the trees in it.

The details once more suggest that a symbolic interpretation is appropriate. The windows of Aseneth's chamber, facing in three directions, indicate that all of creation is visible from eternity. Aseneth's isolation signifies both the soul's isolation in the "tower" of the human form, as well as the untouched purity of the soul with God. The "garden" around the house symbolizes the creation. The seventy-two "young men-at-arms" (four times eighteen at each gate) probably represent the seventy-two nations of the world according to traditional Jewish thought of the time.[16] They would thus signify the entire creation.

The description of the garden, with its ever flowing stream of water passing through, is reminiscent of the garden of Eden in *Genesis,* where the garden "planted eastward in Eden"[17] represents the higher heavenly realms. Consciously or unconsciously, the writer must have drawn upon this image. It seems to have been suggested to the translators of both the Syriac and Latin versions, too, for in these versions, the "spring of water" has become a "spring of *living* water". Living Water from the eternal Spring or Fountain of the Lord are common Middle Eastern metaphors for the 'flow' of the Creative Word throughout creation.

There are many similar scriptural allusions throughout

the story, as well as other similarities to biblical and allied texts, especially in the use of idioms and cultural motifs of the time. But to mention them all seems unnecessary in an exposition of this nature.

II. Joseph

You shall be a Bride to Him

Now it came to pass in the first year of the seven years of plenty, in the fourth month, on the eighteenth of the month, that Joseph arrived in the district of Heliopolis, gathering surplus corn. And as he came near the city, Joseph sent twelve men ahead of him to Pentephres, the priest of Heliopolis, saying, "I will be your guest today, for it is near noon and the time of the midday meal; the sun's heat is overpowering, and I would take rest in the shade of your house."

When Pentephres heard this, he was overjoyed and said, "Blessed be the Lord God of Joseph because my lord Joseph has considered me worthy of a visit." And Pentephres called the steward of his house and said to him, "Make haste and put my house in order, and prepare a fine dinner, because Joseph the Powerful One of God, is coming to us today."

When Aseneth heard that her father and mother had returned from their family estate, she rejoiced and said, "I will go and see my father and my mother for they have returned from our country estate," for it was harvest time. And Aseneth hurried into her chamber and put on a fine linen robe of hyacinth woven with gold, and tied a golden girdle round her waist; and she put bracelets on her hands and golden buskins on her feet. And around her neck she placed a necklace of great price, with precious stones hanging from all sides. And the names of the Egyptian gods were inscribed everywhere, on the bracelets and on the

stones; and the images of the idols were painted on them.
And she put a tiara on her head, fastened a diadem around
her temples, and covered her head with a light veil.

Somehow, Pentephres, though described as an Egyptian
priest and presumably a proponent of Egyptian polytheism,
recognizes Joseph as a worshipper of the one God, whom
Pentephres himself also seems to acknowledge. Aseneth,
however, is depicted as a spoilt child of Egyptian parentage,
a heathen worshipper of Egyptian gods. It is evident that the
writer of *Joseph and Aseneth* sometimes finds the require-
ments of his theme to be in conflict with the dictates of the
biblical characters and narrative he has chosen to embellish!
This is true, however the story is interpreted.

And she made haste and descended the stairs from her
upper floor; and she came to her father and mother, kissing
them in greeting. And Pentephres and his wife were
overjoyed to see their daughter Aseneth adorned and
beautified as a bride of God. And they got out all the good
things they had brought from their country estate, and they
gave them to their daughter. And Aseneth rejoiced at the
good things, and at the fruit, the grapes and the dates, and
at the peaches, the pomegranates and the figs, for they were
all delightful and good to eat.

And Pentephres said to his daughter Aseneth, "My child".
She said, "Behold, here I am, my lord."

And he said to her, "Sit down between us: and I will tell
you what I have to say." And Aseneth sat between her father
and her mother, and her father Pentephres took her right
hand in his right hand and kissed it tenderly and said,
"Aseneth, my child".

And Aseneth said, "What is it, father?"

And Pentephres her father said to her, "Joseph, the
Powerful One of God, is coming to us today, and he is ruler
of all the land of Egypt, for the king Pharaoh has appointed
him ruler of all our land. And he is the administrator of

corn throughout the country and is to save it from the famine that is to come. And this Joseph is a man that worships God: he is self-controlled and a virgin, as are you today, and he is a man of great wisdom and knowledge, and the Spirit of God is upon him, and the grace of the Lord is with him.

"So come, my child, and I will hand you over to him to be his wife. You shall be a bride to him, and he shall be your bridegroom forevermore."

The theme of the bride and bridegroom is now introduced, common mystic imagery for the soul and the Master or Creative Word. The mystic union of the two is, naturally, an eternal union. Hence, the marriage will be "forevermore". Aseneth, however, is not impressed:

When Aseneth heard what her father had to say, her face broke out in a great red sweat. She was furiously angry and looked askance at her father, saying, "Why does my lord and my father speak like this, talking as if he would hand me over like a prisoner to a man of another race, a man who was a fugitive and was sold as a slave? Is not this the shepherd's son from the land of Canaan? Is not this the man who lay with his mistress, and his lord cast him into the prison of darkness, and Pharaoh brought him out of prison because he interpreted his dream, just like old Egyptian women interpret them? No! I will be married to the king's first-born son, for he is king of all Egypt."

On hearing this, Pentephres thought it wiser to say no more to his daughter concerning Joseph, for she had answered him arrogantly and in anger.

Aseneth rejects her father's suggestion outright, recalling the past history of Joseph, related inaccurately with the prejudice of an Egyptian against the Hebrews. But her father keeps quiet at the tantrums of his teenage daughter. (So what's new?)

Joseph is Standing at our Garden Gates

Just then, a young man, one of Pentephres' servants, ran in and said to him, "Behold, Joseph is standing at our garden gates." When Aseneth heard him say this concerning Joseph, she fled from the presence of her father and mother. She ran upstairs and went into her chamber; and she stood at the big window that looked east, in order to see Joseph as he entered her father's house.

And Pentephres, his wife and all his family and servants went out to meet Joseph. The gates to the garden that looked east were opened, and Joseph entered, sitting in Pharaoh's second chariot, drawn by four horses yoked together, white as snow, with golden bridles; and the chariot was fashioned from pure gold. And Joseph was dressed in a marvellous white tunic, and the robe that was wrapped round him was purple, made of fine linen woven with gold, and a golden crown was upon his head, and round the crown were twelve precious stones, and above the stones twelve golden rays; and in his right hand was a royal staff. And in his left he held outstretched an olive branch, bearing a profusion of fruit, and in the fruit was an abundance of oil.

Aseneth runs off in an upset state of mind, having declared that she does not want to know anything about Joseph. All the same, she is intrigued to see what he looks like. So she stands looking out of the east-facing window, the direction from which Joseph will appear. Since the sun dawns in the east, bringing physical light to the world, the east, in mystic language, commonly signifies the 'direction' from which spiritual light arises. Joseph, then, the man of God, enters from the east – and Aseneth looks towards the east to see him.

Aseneth's attitude of apparent rejection, tinged with hidden interest, reflects the condition of a soul who outwardly rejects the spiritual path when first encountered, but is nevertheless attracted and interested.

Joseph is portrayed as the purest of the pure. His horses are as "white as snow", his "chariot is fashioned from pure gold", he is dressed in a "marvellous white tunic", and his robe is of the finest "linen woven with gold". The writer goes beyond the descriptions of *Genesis* and, although his dress is probably traditional royal attire,[18] in this instance it also represents the pristine garment of the pure soul. In fact, as becomes even clearer later on, Joseph represents the Master, an incarnation of the *Logos*. The conveyance of a Master, the Power by which he moves, is the *Logos*. Hence, Joseph's chariot is made of gold, traditionally the richest and most incorruptible of materials, and it is drawn by the whitest of white horses, signifying the utter purity and perfection of the Word.

On his head, Joseph wears a crown set with "twelve precious stones" and "twelve golden rays", characteristic of the Greek sun-god, Helios, considered by the ancients to drive his chariot daily across the sky. The author is not equating Joseph with the sun-god, but is depicting him as a great light, like the "sun from heaven". Perhaps the twelve stones and twelve rays are also intended to suggest the twelve tribes of Israel. Or they may be a metaphor for the twelve *aeons* or primary powers in creation, according to some gnostic schools of thought.[19] The crown also signifies that Joseph is a king, one of the many Middle Eastern epithets for the Master, as well as for God himself.

Even more symbolically, Joseph carries a "royal staff" or king's sceptre "in his right hand". The staff or sceptre is the insignia of royalty[20] – in this case, of the spiritual king or Saviour. Mystically, the staff of wood symbolizes the Tree of Life as the creative Power. It appears in the Mandaean allegory of the *Fisher of Souls*,[21] for instance, and in a number of other places.[22]

In his left hand, he holds, "an olive branch, bearing a profusion of fruit, and in the fruit was an abundance of oil". The olive branch is an ancient symbol of peace and good-will, carried by ambassadors – here, the divine Ambassador or Messenger, the Saviour. Bearing fruit laden with rich oil, it is also a metaphor for the Word, the source of spiritual peace and abundance. Oil was also commonly used as a symbol of wealth, in this case the spiritual wealth of the Tree of Life or Creative Word.[23]

> And Joseph entered the garden and the gates were shut, and all strangers, men or women, remained outside the garden, because the gatekeepers had closed the gates and all strangers were excluded. And Pentephres, his wife, and all his family, except their daughter Aseneth, came and made obeisance to Joseph with their faces upon the ground. And Joseph descended from his chariot, and extended his right hand to them in greeting.

After Joseph has entered, the gates are closed behind him and only members of Pentephres' family and household are allowed to remain inside. That is to say, at the marriage of the soul to the *Logos*, nothing else can be admitted. The mind must be completely pure and one-pointed in its devotion and love for the Lord and his Word. Nothing else should be permitted to enter the mind.

The significance of Joseph's "right hand" becomes clearer towards the end of the story.

When Aseneth saw Joseph

> Now, when Aseneth saw Joseph, her soul was deeply touched, her heart was moved, her insides turned over, her knees became limp, and her whole body trembled. She was awestruck, and sighed, saying:

> > "What can I do now, wretch that I am?
> > Hidden counsellors deceived me, saying,
> > > 'Joseph is coming, (he who is but)
> > > a shepherd's son from the land of Canaan.'

And now, behold, the sun from heaven
　　has come to us in his chariot;
And has entered our house today,
　　and shines in it like a light upon the earth.
But I, being foolish and reckless, despised him,
　　and spoke evil of him,
　　and did not realize that Joseph is a Son of God.
For who among men could ever father such beauty,
　　and what mother could ever give birth to such light?
Wretched am I and foolish,
　　for I spoke evil of him to my father.
"And now, where shall I go,
　　and where can I hide from his presence,
　　lest Joseph, the Son of God, should see me,
　　for I have spoken evil of him?
Where can I flee and hide myself,
　　for he sees every hiding place and knows all things;
And nothing hidden escapes him,
　　by reason of the great light that is within him?
And now may the God of Joseph bestow grace upon me,
　　for I only spoke evil out of ignorance.

"Now, therefore, let my father give me to Joseph
　　as a maidservant and a slave,
　　and I will serve him forevermore."

As soon as Aseneth sees Joseph, she recognizes him as a "Son of God", a Saviour, and is conscious of his "light". He is the "sun from heaven" who has come to the 'City of the Sun' (Heliopolis). She is also aware of his "beauty", traditional since the *Genesis* story. "For who among men could ever father such beauty?" is an acknowledgement that the spiritual father of a Son of God is (naturally) the Lord. He is the one who sends such souls to this world, infusing them with his beauty. Spiritually, they are born of his essence, though their human forms are born in the usual manner.

Aseneth also regrets the things she said before, realizing

that Joseph, as a Master, is all-knowing and all-seeing. "For he sees every hiding place and knows all things." Knowledge of hidden things, human and divine, was as commonly ascribed to the true prophet as to God himself. As the first-century Jewish commentator of Alexandria, Philo Judaeus, wrote:

> To a prophet nothing is unknown, since he has within him a spiritual sun (light) and unclouded rays to give him a full and clear apprehension of things unseen by sense, but apprehended by the understanding.
>
> *Philo, On the Special Laws IV:36; cf. PCW8 p.127*

So Aseneth hopes for Joseph's grace, compassion and under-standing of her ignorance, and is -- according to the story -- immediately humbled, wishing only to be his maidservant and slave. Like the prodigal son in the well-known parable of Jesus, awareness of her condition diminishes her expectations in preparation for her receiving far more. Such is the grace of God.

All this is indicative of the author's representation of Joseph as the highest kind of prophet – a perfect Master or Saviour, the Word made flesh.[24] For although Joseph is portrayed in *Genesis* as a person of great beauty, he is depicted more as a good and spiritual man than a great prophet, though there may also be some allegorical meaning hidden in the *Genesis* story of Jacob, Joseph and his eleven brothers. That Aseneth wishes to be his "maidservant" or "slave" indicates the attitude of the true disciple who has surrendered his or her individual self or ego to the Master, considering themselves to be his servant.

The writer of this story is not alone in portraying Joseph as a holy man, above that of the *Genesis* description. In the *Wisdom of Solomon,* a Greek text from mid-first century BC, the writer describes Wisdom as the creative Power, man's ever present guiding spirit, the companion of holy men and the essential guide to many of the Jewish prophets and patriarchs. Among these holy men, he includes Jacob and his son Joseph:

> Wisdom delivered her servants from their ordeals.
> The upright man (Jacob),
> > fleeing from the anger of his brother,
> > was led by her along straight paths.
> She (Wisdom) showed him the kingdom of God
> > and taught him the knowledge of holy things....
>
> She did not forsake the upright man (Joseph)
> > when he was sold, but kept him free from sin;
> She accompanied him down into the pit;
> Nor did she abandon him in his chains,
> > until she had procured for him the sceptre of a kingdom
> > and authority over his despotic masters;
> Thus exposing as liars those who had traduced him,
> > and giving him honour everlasting.
>
> *Wisdom of Solomon 10:9–10, 13–14; cf. NJB*

The writer is allegorizing the stories of the prophets and patriarchs of traditional Jewish history. "She showed him the kingdom of God and taught him the knowledge of holy things" refers to the inner knowledge of true mystics. The "dungeon" is this world, while the king's "sceptre" is a symbol of the power given by God to a true prophet, Master or Saviour.

When Joseph saw Aseneth

So Joseph entered the house of Pentephres and sat upon a seat (of honour); and they washed his feet and placed a separate table in front of him, because Joseph never ate with the Egyptians, for that was an abomination to him. And looking up, Joseph saw Aseneth leaning through (the window). And he said to Pentephres and his family, "Who is that woman standing by the window of the upper floor? Let her leave this house."

This was because Joseph was concerned, thinking, "Lest she solicit me"; for all the wives and daughters of the noblemen and satraps of all the land of Egypt used to solicit him in order that they might lie with him. And all the wives and daughters of the Egyptians, as many as saw Joseph, were greatly disturbed on account of his beauty. But Joseph rebuffed them. And the emissaries they sent to him with gold and silver and valuable gifts, Joseph would reject out of hand (*lit.* with threats and insults), saying, "I will not sin in the sight of the Lord God and in the face of my father Jacob." And Joseph kept the face of his father Jacob (*var.* God) continually before his eyes, and he remembered his father's commandments. For Jacob used to say to Joseph and his brothers, "Be firmly on your guard, my children, against associating with a strange woman, and have nothing to do with her, for association with her is ruin and destruction." That is why Joseph said, "Tell that woman to leave this house."

And Pentephres said to him, "My lord, the woman you have seen standing in the upper floor is no strange woman; she is our daughter, a virgin, who recoils from men; and no other man has ever seen her, apart from you today. And if you wish it, she shall come and speak with you; for our daughter is as a sister to you."

And Joseph was overjoyed because Pentephres had said, "She is a virgin who recoils from men." And Joseph said to himself, "If she is a virgin who recoils from men, she will certainly not solicit me." And he said to Pentephres and his wife, "If she is your daughter and a virgin, then let her come; for she is my sister, and from today I will consider (*lit.* love) her as my sister."

Joseph is welcomed into the house of Pentephres in a traditional manner. He is given a seat of honour and his feet are washed. Among pupils, family members and other dependants, washing the feet of their respective masters was an accepted custom. Here, it symbolizes Joseph's position as a spiritual Master.

For Joseph not to eat with "Egyptians" because "this was an abomination to him" reflects Jewish custom of the time, particularly relevant to Jews living in the pagan world, away from Palestine. However, the *Exodus* story of the children of Israel, freed from captivity in Egypt (the physical universe) and led to the promised land (the eternal realm) by the Saviour Moses, was also understood as a gnostic allegory. Thus, the children of Israel and, by extension, the Jewish people, represent those who are following the path that leads to God, while the Egyptians signify the people of the world.

The author of the present story is therefore reinforcing his point that Joseph is not a man of this world. He is not an 'Egyptian'. He is indicating that a Master does not come to mix with all the people of this world, but only to collect those souls, the 'children of Israel', who have been allocated or chosen for him.[25]

Joseph then sees Aseneth looking at him through an upstairs window. The ensuing explanation, possibly a later addition to the original story, is based upon the Jewish and Christian legend that all the Egyptian women who encountered Joseph on his travels around Egypt were inescapably attracted by his beauty, offering him rich gifts in the hope of soliciting his attention.[26] Joseph, for his part, received strength to resist them either from the memory of his father or by his father's personal intervention and appearance. The story serves to underline both Joseph's beauty and also his great purity and freedom from temptation, both hallmarks of a truly holy man.

The admonition not to associate with a "strange woman", found throughout biblical and allied literature,[27] is usually an injunction against marrying a non-Jew[28] unless she converts to Judaism. 'Strange' here means 'foreign' or 'alien'. But like Joseph's refusal to eat with the Egyptians, 'strange' also refers to a person or woman of the world, particularly one who has ulterior designs. In fact, in *Proverbs,* the "strange woman" is depicted more as a harlot than as a non-Jew. She is also described as the antithesis of Wisdom, and is depicted in such a way that she would seem to be a metaphor for the illusion and deception of the world:

> To Wisdom say, "My sister!"
> Call Perception (Wisdom) your dearest friend,
>   to preserve you from the alien (strange) woman,
>   from the stranger, with her wheedling words....
> And now, my son, listen to me,
>   pay attention to the words I have to say:
> Do not let your heart stray into her ways,
>   or wander into her paths;
> She has done so many to death,
>   and the strongest have all been her victims.
> Her house is the way to Sheol,
>   the descent to the courts of death.
>
>   *Proverbs 7:4–5, 24–27, JB*

The personification of the illusion and deception of this world as a woman is common in Oriental thought. "She has done so many to death" refers to spiritual death, while "Sheol" and the "courts of death" refer as much to this world as to any hellish region.[29]

Greet your Brother

So Aseneth's mother went up to the upper floor and brought Aseneth down and presented her to Joseph. And Pentephres said to his daughter, "Greet your brother, for he too is a virgin as are you today, and he recoils from all strange women just as you recoil from all strange men."

And Aseneth said to Joseph, "May you have joy, my lord, you who are blessed by God Most High."

And Joseph said to her, "May God, who gives life to all things, bless you."

And Pentephres said to Aseneth, "Draw near and kiss your brother."

And when she drew near to kiss Joseph, Joseph stretched out his right hand and laid it on her chest, between her two breasts, saying, "It is not fitting for a man who worships God, who with his mouth glorifies the living God, and eats the blessed Bread of Life, and drinks the blessed Cup of Immortality, and is anointed with the blessed Unction (Oil) of Incorruption, to kiss a strange woman, who with her mouth glorifies dumb and lifeless idols, and eats from their table the bread of strangulation, and drinks from their libation the cup of deceit, and is anointed with the unction of destruction.

"A man who worships God will kiss his mother and the sister who is born of his mother and the sister who is of his own tribe and kin, and the wife that shares his bed, and who all with their mouths glorify the Living God.

"Likewise, for a woman who worships God it is not fitting to kiss a strange man, because this is an abomination in the sight of the Lord God."

Joseph's holiness is again emphasized and the reason for it is now explicitly stated. He "glorifies the Living God, and eats the blessed Bread of Life, and drinks the blessed Cup of Immortality, and is anointed with the blessed Unction (Oil) of Incorruption". The "Living God" means that God is the one Source of all life and being, while the "Bread of Life", the "Cup of Immortality" and the "Unction of Incorruption" are common metaphors in the ancient literature for the Creative Word.

A true Saviour is one with this great Power; he is a personification or incarnation of it. It is his lifeblood, so to speak. His life is drawn from it, and he subsists in it. Therefore, it can be said that he eats the "Bread of Life", drinks from the "Cup of Immortality" and is anointed, in the manner of ancient Middle Eastern kings and Jewish high priests, with the 'holy oil' of the Word – the "Unction of Incorruption".[30] Mystically, he is the spiritual king and the highest of all 'high priests'.

The soul who is engrossed with this world is described as a "strange woman". The "dumb and lifeless idols" whom she glorifies are the idols of pagan gods, made of earthly materials, possessing neither life nor life-giving properties. Metaphorically, they are also the dead material things of physical existence that we worship and glorify by giving our complete attention to them, as if they were the beginning and end of everything. More generally, the "strange woman" also personifies the illusion of material life.

The "bread of strangulation", eaten from the table of these gods, alludes to the pagan practice of sacrificing animals to the gods before eating them. Meat is called the food of death, not only because it is procured by the taking of life, but also because it brings about spiritual death through incurring a heavy burden of karma or sin. Metaphorically, the "bread of strangulation" is also the food of absorption in the physical senses and worldly activity.

Drinking the "libation" offered to these gods is similarly described as a "cup of deceit" because alcohol creates a cloudiness in the mind and incites the senses, leading to degradation of character and the loss of spiritual understanding. As the writer of *Proverbs* puts it, also expressing a vegetarian inclination:

> Be not among the winebibbers, nor among those
>   who gorge themselves with meat (*lit.* flesh);
> For the drunkard and glutton impoverish themselves,
>   and a drowsy head makes a wearer of rags.
>
> *Proverbs 23:20–21; cf. JB, KJV*

Metaphorically, drinking from the "cup" of idol worship, as well as from the "cup" of worldliness, leads to a state of delusion regarding the true nature of reality. The soul becomes lost in the "deceit" or illusion of the world, and forgets her true spiritual purpose and the Living God who dwells within.

The "strange woman" or soul lost in this world is also "anointed with the unction of destruction". This contrasts with the "Unction of Incorruption". "Incorruption", here, means that which is eternal and not liable to change or decay. "Destruction" refers to that which changes and is liable to dissolution and death – that is, to the things and bodies of this world.

A "kiss" – which Joseph at this point refuses to share with Aseneth – is a common symbol of union, either of mystic union with God or of material 'union' with this world. It is said in the *Talmud* that Moses, Aaron and Miriam all died of a kiss from God.[31] The meaning, of course, is spiritual. Their death is death to this world, withdrawal of all consciousness from this world, and the kiss from God refers to the touch of divine grace that draws the soul out of the body. This interpretation appears in the medieval *Zohar*, as explained by the nineteenth-century scholar, Adolphe Franck:

> "In one of the most mysterious and most exalted parts of heaven there is a palace of love. The most profound mysteries are there; there are all souls well-beloved by the celestial King, the Holy One, praised be he, together with the holy spirits with whom he unites by kisses of love."[32] Hence, the death of the righteous is referred to as God's kiss.... This kiss is the union of the soul with the Substance (Source) from which it springs.
>
> *Adolphe Franck, KRPH p.136*

Kisses also appear metaphorically in the biblical *Song of Songs*, where the lover (the soul) says to the divine Beloved:

> Let him kiss me with the kisses of his mouth.
> Your love is more delightful than wine; ...
> We shall praise your love above wine;
> How right it is to love you.
>
> *Song of Songs 1:2, 4, JB*

In the present story, by refusing to kiss Aseneth, still in her state of worldliness and impurity, the author means that Joseph, as a Son of God, cannot be mystically united to a soul held captive by materiality. Or, more generally, a Master is not attracted by the illusion of transient phenomena. At the mundane level, the writer also adds that kissing family members is acceptable because it generally conveys no underlying inducement to temptation.

Joseph's Blessing

When Aseneth heard what Joseph said, she was grieved and greatly distressed and sighed; and as she kept gazing steadfastly at Joseph with open eyes, they filled with tears. And when Joseph saw her weeping, his heart went out to her – for he was tender-hearted and compassionate and feared the Lord. Then, raising his right hand and placing it upon her head, he said:

"Lord God of my father Israel,
  the Most High, the Powerful One of Jacob,
Who gives life to all things,
  and has called them from darkness to light,
  and from Error unto Truth,
  and from death to Life:
Do you, O Lord, bless this virgin, and quicken her,
  and renew her with your Holy Spirit;
And remould her by your hidden Hand,
  and make her alive again with your Life.
And may she eat your Bread of Life,
  and may she drink your Cup of Blessing.

"And number her among your people
  whom you chose before all things came into being.
And may she enter into your rest,
  which you have prepared for your chosen ones.
And may she dwell in your eternal life forevermore."

Although Aseneth is disturbed and distressed by Joseph's attitude, at the same time she is enraptured by his presence and his great beauty: "She kept gazing steadfastly at Joseph with open eyes." Tender-hearted as Masters are, Joseph is moved to compassion and blesses Aseneth, unmindful of her previous rejection of him. The time is not yet ripe for the mystic union of the soul with the *Logos*, but his blessing will prepare her.

God is described as the Source of life, the One who can lead a soul from the "darkness" of this world to the light of God, from the "Error" or illusion of materiality into the "Truth" that is God, from the death of living in this world to the free and blissful life of the spirit in the higher realms and with God.

Joseph calls down a real and inward blessing upon Aseneth. Joseph's "right hand", "your hidden Hand", "your Holy Spirit",[33] "your Life",[34] "your Bread of Life", "your Cup of Blessing" are all allusions to the Creative Word, the *Logos*, by which a Master gives his spiritual blessing. This is no religious hyperbole, unctuous sentiment or expression of a vague religious hope. A Master's blessing is more real than any physical gift of this world, touching the soul in the core of her being.

The terms "Hand" and "Right Hand" are found throughout Judaic literature as metaphors for God's Creative Word, as in *Isaiah*, when Yahweh 'says':

> I ... am the first, I am also the last.
> My Hand laid the foundations of the earth
>   and my Right Hand spread out the heavens.
>
> *Isaiah 48:12–13, NJB*

"Your Right Hand" also appears in the *Psalms:*[35]

> Yours are the heavens, and yours the earth:
>   you founded the world and all it holds;
> The north and the south, you have created them....

Yours is a mighty arm:
    strong your Hand, exalted your Right Hand.

Psalms 89:11–13; cf. KJV, NJB

And:

I meditate on you all night long,
    for you have always helped me.
I sing for joy in the shadow of your wings;
    my soul clings close to you,
    your Right Hand supports me.

Psalms 63:7–8, JB

In the Manichaean psalms in Coptic, the devotee speaks at one place of the "Living Spirit, our first Right Hand",[36] and at another of the protection and blessing afforded by God's "Right Hand":

In a moment, my God, your mercy became one with me.
Because of your strong protection,
    lo, my diseases passed far from me.
Lo, joy has overtaken me
    through your Right Hand that came to me.

Manichaean Psalm Book; cf. MPB p.153

One of the gnostic writers is even more explicit. He says that this "Hand of the Lord" has created everything:

Only the Hand of the Lord has created all these things.
For this Hand of the Father ... forms all.

Teachings of Silvanus 115, NHS30 pp.360–61

The right hand is usually the strongest and most dexterous hand, and is a common and quite general idiom. In these and other instances, however, the metaphor is clearly more specific.

Joseph also prays that Aseneth may be numbered among

"your people, whom you chose before all things came into being." "Your people" who have been chosen from the beginning are those souls have been ordained by God to be collected or rescued by a particular Saviour and taken back to him, whenever the time is right.[37]

The soul will then "enter into your rest, which you have prepared for your chosen ones". "Rest" is a common term in Judaic and Christian literature.[38] It refers to the peace and bliss of the soul when it reaches the eternity of God, the everlasting Source of life and being, beyond all time, space and separation. It is there that the soul attains true spiritual salvation or redemption.

Now Aseneth was filled with joy at Joseph's blessing and, hastening, she returned to her upper floor and fell on her bed exhausted; for she felt not only happiness, but also sorrow and great awe and trembling. And she had been perspiring continuously since she had heard Joseph speak these words to her in the name of God Most High. And she wept greatly and bitterly, and she repented on account of her gods whom she used to worship, and she spurned all the idols and waited for evening to come.

And Joseph ate and drank, and told his servants, "Yoke the horses to the chariot". For he said, "I must depart and visit all of this land."

And Pentephres said to Joseph, "Lodge here today, my lord, and continue on your way tomorrow."

But Joseph said, "No! I must depart now, for this is the day on which God began to make all his creatures. But in eight days time, when this day returns, I also will return to you and lodge here."

Naturally, Aseneth is overjoyed to receive Joseph's blessing, especially since she had previously rejected and spoken ill of him. But the effect he has on her is overwhelming, reflecting the inner dance of joy that the soul feels when she comes into contact with a Master after being lost for ages in the labyrinth of creation. Deep and intense emotions can flood through a person when they come into contact with a spiritualized being of this calibre. At the deepest of all levels, the soul recognizes intuitively who the Master really is, and this can be reflected at the human level as powerful but mixed feelings – bliss, weeping, sighing, guilt, awe, feelings of unworthiness and a desire for a change in the direction of one's life.

Joseph, for his part, decides to leave right away and return "in eight days time" – after the lapse of seven days. Through the dialogue, the writer makes a particular point of this, and it is clearly intended to be understood symbolically. According to one of the two creation myths in *Genesis,* God began creation on a Sunday. On the seventh day, the following Saturday or Sabbath, God 'rested' (whatever that may mean). The eighth day, therefore, is the first real Sunday, the first day of creation.

For Aseneth to have to wait until the first day of a new creation symbolizes the period required for her acceptance of and preparation for a new way of life, before her renewal, rebirth, mystic baptism or initiation. A person generally takes some time to absorb a Master's message and come to terms with it within themselves. Usually, a period of far longer than seven days would be required for such a readjustment. We are in the realms of symbolism and storytelling, however, and seven days is all Aseneth is going to get!

III. The Repentance of Aseneth

Aseneth was left Alone

So Joseph departed, and Pentephres and his relations left for their estate, while Aseneth was left alone with the seven virgins, oppressed and weeping until the sun set. She neither ate bread nor drank water. And when night fell, while everyone else slept, she alone remained awake, continuing to weep, often beating her breast with her hand, filled with a sense of awe, and trembling greatly.

Then Aseneth arose from her bed and, creeping softly down the stairs from the upper floor, went to the gate house where she found the gatekeeper asleep with her children. And Aseneth swiftly took down the leather curtain from the doorway and, filling it with ashes from the fireplace, she carried it to her upper floor and laid it on the floor. Then she closed the door securely, slipping an iron bolt across. And she sighed deeply and wept bitterly.

Now the virgin whom Aseneth loved most of all the virgins heard her sighing and, hastening, she roused the six other virgins. And they went to Aseneth's door and found it locked. And hearing Aseneth sighing and weeping, they stood outside, saying, "What is it, my lady, and why are you so sorrowful? What is it that is troubling you? Open to us, so that we can see how you are."

But Aseneth did not open the door. From within, she said to them, "I have a dreadful headache and am resting on my bed; and I do not have the strength in my limbs to rise and open the door to you, for I am utterly exhausted. But go each of you to her own chamber and sleep, and let me be still." And the virgins went away, each to her own chamber.

Using conventional images of the times (beating of the breast and so on), the writer describes Aseneth's condition of emotion and her desire for repentance. She remains on her own; she fasts; and she is in a disturbed state of mind. Then, while everyone is asleep, she slips downstairs, stealthily collects some ashes from the gatekeeper's fire and quietly returns to her room. When her seven girlfriends hear her sobbing, they come to find out what the matter is, but she makes the perennial excuse of a bad headache, and tells them not to worry.

Then Aseneth arose and softly opened her door, and went into her second chamber where her treasure chests and ornaments were, and she opened her coffer and took out a black and sombre tunic. This was her mourning tunic which she had worn when her eldest brother had died. And she took her black tunic and carried it into her chamber, and closed the door securely again, slipping the bolt across.

And Aseneth hastened and took off her royal robe of linen woven with gold, and dressed in the black tunic of mourning. She loosed her golden girdle and tied a rope around her waist instead, and she took her tiara and the diadem from her head, and the bracelets from her hands and feet, and laid everything on the floor. Then she took her best robe, and the golden girdle and the tiara and the diadem, and threw them all through the north-facing window for the poor.

And Aseneth hastened and took all the gods that were in her chamber, the innumerable ones of gold and silver, and broke them into fragments, and she threw all the idols of the Egyptians out of the north-facing window of her upper floor for the poor people and beggars.

Aseneth now proceeds to destroy or at least get rid of all the things that symbolize her previous life. She divests herself of all the finery of which she was previously so proud, and puts on a dull black dress: she detaches herself from all the paraphernalia of the world and dons a garment of humility, one of which she cannot feel vain. Black garments were commonly worn in Jewish tradition by those in mourning or to indicate repentance. So, too, were they worn as mourning in Greek and Roman circles, though not – interestingly – in Egyptian culture. The sudden appearance of an elder brother seems to be an invention of the author, for – like many other aspects of the narrative – there is no brother in the Bible story nor in any other allied writings. It simply provides a reason for Aseneth's possession of a black mourning dress.

Aseneth also gives all her precious garments and ornaments to the "poor". They are thrown through the "north-facing window", the direction from which the sun does not shine and the light never enters. The "poor" symbolize the people of the world, devoid of spiritual light and stricken by spiritual poverty. They are the ones who give a value to such ostentation. Perhaps Aseneth's actions also indicate that generosity and giving to the needy are a necessary part of the spiritual life she is about to adopt, as in the advice of Jesus to some who wanted to follow him.[39]

Likewise, she discards all her previous forms of worship. They, too, are summarily dispatched through the "north-facing window", this time for "beggars" as well as the "poor". Obsession with the world makes an already poor person into a beggar, always hankering and asking for more and more.

> Then Aseneth took her royal dinner, even the fatted beasts and the fish and the flesh of the heifer, and all the sacrifices to her gods, and the wine vessels for their libations; and she threw everything out of the north-facing window as food for stray dogs. For Aseneth said to herself, "By no means should my dogs eat from my dinner and from the idol sacrifices, but let the stray dogs eat those."

She also disposes of her animal sacrifices and alcoholic drinks in the same manner. They all go through the same window as "food for stray dogs" – she does not even want her own dogs to eat them. As well as decrying the custom of sacrificing animals to the gods and the pouring of alcoholic drinks in their 'honour', the writer may also be indicating that the followers of the higher mystic path also give up the use of animal food and alcoholic drink. There are many references in the literature of all ages and cultures to the vegetarian and teetotal diets of followers of the mystic or gnostic path.[40] Like the "poor people and beggars", "stray dogs" are an allusion to the people of the world. They roam around without any real sense of direction, and have no true home.

There must have been more than a few surprises in store for the passers-by that day. Let us hope that Aseneth checked where she was throwing things before bidding them farewell!

After this, Aseneth took the leather curtain containing the ashes and poured them on the floor. And she took a piece of sackcloth and wrapped it around her waist, and she loosed the fillet from the hair of her head and sprinkled ashes over her head. Then she also scattered ashes on the floor, and fell down upon the ashes and, striking her breast repeatedly with her two hands, she wept bitterly, sighing and moaning all night until dawn.

When Aseneth arose at daybreak, and looked, behold the ashes beneath her were like mud because of her tears. Then Aseneth again fell down on her face upon the ashes until the setting of the sun. And so Aseneth did for seven days. And she ate no bread and drank no water in those seven days of the passion of her soul and of her self-abasement.

Using contemporary Jewish cultural images associated with mourning and repentance – sackcloth and ashes, untying the hair, beating of the breast, weeping and fasting – the writer now conveys the turmoil in Aseneth's mind as she realizes the futility of her previous way of life, and seeks to destroy her pride and egotism. She does this for "seven" days, seven and seventy being traditional numbers in the religious mythology of Judaism and the ancient Middle East. In the apocryphal *2 Baruch,* for instance, as well as *4 Ezra,* a sequence of seven-day fasts, accompanied by mourning and prayer, precede revelational experiences.[41] As before, the writer of *Joseph and Aseneth* is drawing on cultural and literary motifs with which he is familiar.

IV. THE PRAYERS OF ASENETH

With whom shall I Seek Refuge?

On the eighth day, when dawn had come and birds were already singing and dogs were barking at passers-by, Aseneth lifted up her head a little from the floor and the ashes on which she was lying, for she was very weak and had lost control of her limbs because of her fasting and abstinence and self-abasement. And she rose onto her knees, and put her hands on the floor, and lifted herself up a little from the floor, with her head bowed, while the hair of her head hung in strands from the weight of ashes. And Aseneth clasped her hands, finger against finger, and shook her head to and fro, and struck her breast repeatedly with her two hands. And her face was flooded with tears, and she sighed deeply, pulling the hair from her head and pouring on ashes.

In short, Aseneth is a mess, inside and out. Employing an assortment of traditional mourning and repentance images, the writer continues to describe Aseneth's state of mind and body.

And Aseneth was tired and faint, and her strength was failing. And she turned to face the wall, and she sat below the east-facing window. And she laid her head on her bosom, clasping the fingers of her hands around her right knee; and her mouth was closed for she had not opened it during the seven days and the seven nights of her self-abasement.

In a desperation and yearning that she herself can hardly understand, Aseneth turns to the east, symbolizing the source of spiritual light, and she now expresses her thoughts in a silent, unspoken prayer, representing her innermost feelings. The narrative at this point, as well as the content of Aseneth's subsequent prayers, appears to be influenced by the biblical book of *Esther*. Queen Esther also takes off her "sumptuous robes", dresses in "sorrowful mourning", covers her head with "ashes and dung", "humbles her body", tears her hair out and, seeking refuge with God, utters a prayer of forgiveness for her sins.[42] So, too, does Aseneth:

And she said in her heart, not opening her mouth:

"What shall I do, or where shall I go?
With whom shall I seek refuge, or what shall I say? –
  I, the virgin and orphan,
  desolate, forsaken and rejected[43] by all?
Everybody has cast me aside,[44]
  even my father and my mother are among them,
  for I have spurned and rejected their gods
  and have destroyed them,
  causing them to be trodden underfoot by men.
For my father and mother said,
  'Aseneth is not our daughter.'
And all my family, too,
  have cast me aside, and everybody else,
  for I have destroyed their gods.
And I, too, have rejected every man
  and all who asked my hand in marriage.
And now, in my self-abasement,
  I am rejected by all,
  and they gloat over my tribulation.

"And the Lord God of the most powerful Joseph
  rejects[45] all who worship idols,
  because he is a jealous and a terrible God
  towards all who worship strange gods.
Therefore he, too, has rejected me,
  because I worshipped dumb and lifeless idols,
  and glorified them, and have eaten of their sacrifices,
  and my mouth is polluted from their table.

And I do not have the courage
    to call upon the Lord God of heaven, the Most High,
    the Powerful One of the mighty Joseph,
    because my mouth is polluted from eating idol sacrifices.

"But I have heard many say
    that the God of the Hebrews is a true God,
    a Living God and a merciful God,
    and compassionate, long-suffering, merciful and gentle,
    one who does not weigh the sin of a repentant person,
    especially of one who sins in ignorance,
    nor does he condemn the lawless deeds
    of one who suffers, while he is suffering.
"Therefore, I will take courage, too, and turn to him,
    and seek refuge with him,
    and confess all my sins to him,
    and pour out my petition before him.
For who knows, perhaps he will see my low estate,
    and have mercy on me.
Perhaps he will see the desolation of my soul,
    and have compassion on me;
Or see my orphaned state,
    and come to my help.
For he is a father of orphans,
    a helper of the persecuted,
    and a consolation to those who suffer.
Therefore, I will take courage and cry to him."

Aseneth berates herself and feels thoroughly sorry for herself. She has reached the lowest ebb of her life. She now feels that everyone she once knew has rejected her because she has rejected both them and her past beliefs and way of life. She even imagines that her parents have rejected her, which is untrue, since they have great respect for Joseph and all he represents. She also feels that Joseph has rejected her because of the way she used to live. So she feels doubly rejected and, because of these thoughts and her feeling of sinfulness, she cannot find the courage to turn to the "Living God". All this epitomizes the inner turmoil that can accompany true spiritual repentance – a turning of the mind away from the world and towards God.

In the end, however, she realizes that the "Living God" is always described as "compassionate, long-suffering, merciful and gentle, one who does not weigh the sin of a repentant person, especially of one who sins in ignorance". Therefore, she summons up her courage and instead of wallowing in self-pity, she tries to seek his forgiveness. She also presumes that he can see her, will consider her with compassion, and will come to her assistance. Aseneth then frames another silent prayer to give herself the courage to turn to the "merciful God", the introduction following the same formula as before:

> And Aseneth arose from the wall where she was sitting, and turned to the east-facing window, and sat up on her knees, and stretched out her hands towards heaven. And Aseneth was afraid to open her mouth, and to speak to God Most High, and to name the name of God. And she turned again to face the wall and sat, frequently striking her breast and her head with her hands. And she said in her heart, not opening her mouth:

> "Wretched as I am, an orphan and desolate,
>   my mouth is polluted by eating idol sacrifices,
>   and from receiving the blessed gifts
>   of the gods of the Egyptians.
> And now, though I have tortured my body,
>   mingling ashes with my tears,
>   I dare not open my mouth
>   to invoke his terrible and holy name.
> For perhaps the Lord will be angry with me
>   for calling upon his holy name
>   in the midst of my lawless deeds?
> "What then shall I do, wretched as I am?

I will take courage and open my mouth to him,
    and call upon the holy name of the merciful God.
And if in anger the Lord tramples upon me,
    he is himself able to heal me again;
And if he punish me with sufferings,
    in his mercy, he himself can comfort me again,
    and, in punishing me,
    he may renew me through his mercy.
And should he be angry with me for my sins,
    he may be reconciled unto me,
    and pardon all my sins.
Therefore, I will take courage and open my mouth to him."

Her "lawless deeds" are those which contravene the Law. Ostensibly, this is the Jewish Law of Moses, the code of conduct in Judaism, as laid down in the *Pentateuch*. The higher, divine Law, however, is the Creative Word, and a number of the ancient texts make it clear that the real Law referred to by Moses is the mystic Word, not the rules of outer behaviour.[46] Understood mystically, "lawless deeds" are not transgressions of Judaism, but all those thoughts and actions that keep a soul away from the divine Word. These are the real sins that a person commits, and for which an accounting will be exacted by the natural karmic law, the law of recompense for all thought and action, good or bad.

Every thought and action leaves an impression on the mind. Nothing goes unaccounted for in the greater scheme of things. All action originates in the mind: every action has a motive, great or small, conscious or subconscious. And the mind is never still. But its attention can only go in one of two fundamental directions – inwards or outwards.

When the mind goes out, it loses contact with the divine Law or Word within. Then all deeds that come from it are "lawless". This is the normal human condition.

But when the mind develops an inward tendency, when it truly repents in a positive fashion, then it comes into harmony with the higher Law. Then its deeds are no longer "lawless", for its only motivations are love and selflessness. This is the only true repentance.

You Spoke the Word

Aseneth is in the process of making this inner about face. Having summoned up the courage, she now turns openly and in all sincerity to God, symbolized by her speaking her prayer aloud. Once again, she is on her knees. Generally, Jews would have prayed standing up. Prostration or kneeling, as in Aseneth's case, indicate her particular intensity and fervour:

> And Aseneth arose again from the wall where she had been sitting, and sat up on her knees. And she stretched out her hands towards the east, and with her eyes looked up to heaven, and she opened her mouth to God and said:

> > "O Lord, God:
> > Who created all beings and gave life to them,
> >   who gave the Breath of Life to your entire creation,
> >   who brought the Invisible into light (existence),
> >   who made all things;
> > Who has made manifest the Unmanifest,
> >   who has raised heaven (to its place),
> >   and founded the earth upon the waters;
> > Who has fixed huge stones upon the depths of the waters,
> >   which are not submerged,
> >   but remain like oak leaves floating on the water's surface,
> >   and are like living stones that hear your Voice, O Lord,
> >   and keep your Commandments,
> >   which you have given them,
> >   never transgressing your Ordinances,
> >   but to the end are doing your will.

"For you, O Lord, spoke the Word,
   and all things came into being;
And your Word, O Lord, is the life of all your creatures."

God is depicted as the source of all things, animate and inanimate. He has created everything through his "Breath of Life", his "Commandments" or his "Word" – all three being synonymous. Creation by God's Word is an essential principle of both Judaism and Christianity, though often it is little understood. In fact, it is a principle of Islam and most other religions, too. God has made both earth and the heavens (inner and outer) by his "Word" or his "Voice". John's gospel begins with this theme, and refers to it continually, throughout.[47] It is also found in Jewish biblical and allied literature, as in the *Wisdom of Solomon,* written in mid-second century BC:

God of our ancestors, Lord of mercy,
   who by your Word have made all things.
              Wisdom of Solomon 9:1, JB

And in the *Wisdom of Jesus Ben Sirach,* from the same period:

By the Word of the Lord, his works come into being
   and all creation obeys his will....
All things hold together by means of his Word.
              Wisdom of Jesus Ben Sirach 42:15, 43:26, JB

And in the *Psalms,* where the Word is also called the "Breath of his Mouth":

By the Word of Yahweh, the heavens were made,
   their whole array by the Breath of his Mouth.
              Psalms 33:9, JB

Likewise, in the little-known *Judith,* where it is both "your Breath" and "your Voice":

> Lord, you are great, you are glorious,
>   wonderfully strong, unconquerable.
> May your whole creation serve you!
> For you spoke and things came into being;
> You sent your Breath,
>   and they were put together,
>   and no one can resist your Voice.
>
> *Judith 16:13–14, NJB*

Raising the heavens and founding the "earth upon the waters" are a prevalent feature of creation cosmology of that time, adopted into Christianity from Judaism, and derived from *Genesis*.[48] The "waters" are a metaphor for the primeval ocean of the divine Spirit. The formula is often repeated,[49] as in the early Christian *Shepherd of Hermas*, where an 'angel' speaks of the creative power as "his great Wisdom", "his glorious Counsel" and "his mighty Word":

> Lo, the God of the powers, whom I love,
>   by his mighty Power, and by his great Wisdom,
>   created the world;
> And, by his glorious Counsel,
>   surrounded his creation with beauty;
> And, by his mighty Word,
>   fixed the heaven and founded the earth
>   upon the waters.
>
> *Shepherd of Hermas, Visions 1:3:4, AF2 p.15*

There are many other passages, too, throughout the mystic literature of the world, not only of the ancient Middle East, which speak of God's creative power as his Word, his Wisdom and by many other names. It is a characteristic and universal feature of mystic teachings.

The writer of our present text continues that he has also "fixed huge stones upon the depths of the waters, which are not submerged". The "waters" are the stormy waters of this world, surging with the constant movement of the mind, the senses and material things. The "fixed huge stones", which do not sink and "are like living stones", are the Sons of God or Saviours. They are always in the physical creation. They always keep their heads above the stormy waters, and are never in danger of being submerged. They also "hear your Voice, O Lord": they hear the Voice or Word of God within themselves as the sweetest of divine Music. They are in tune with the divine will and hence they are "never transgressing your Ordinances".

The imagery of firm steps set in the chaotic waters or rivers of the world is also found in the early Christian *Odes of Solomon:*

> For the Lord (Messiah) has bridged them by his Word:
> > he has walked over and crossed them on foot.
> And his footsteps remain upon the waters,
> > and have not disappeared,
> > but are like a tree
> > that is firmly fixed (*or* founded on truth).
> On this side and on that,
> > the waves rise up;
> But the footsteps of our Lord Messiah remain,
> > and are neither obliterated nor effaced.
> For a Way has been established
> > for those who cross after him,
> > and for those who follow in the footsteps of his faith,
> > and who adore his Holy Name.
>
> *Odes of Solomon 39:9–13, OSD p.166*

Here, the world is compared to rushing rivers which are bridged by a Saviour. His footprints are of the Word. They become stable, even on the rushing torrent, like "a tree that is firmly secured" (or, in a wordplay, "founded on truth"), providing a path to God for all who follow him.

Aseneth's prayer or lament continues:

With you do I Seek Refuge

"With you, O Lord, do I seek refuge,
  to you, my Master, will I call to hear my petition,
  to you will I confess my sins,
  to you will I reveal my transgressions of your Law.
Spare me, O Lord, for I have sinned greatly in your sight,
  I have transgressed your Law and acted impiously,
  and I have spoken evil and unspeakable things
  in your sight.
My mouth, O Lord, has been polluted
  by eating idol sacrifices,
  and from the table of the gods of the Egyptians.
I have sinned, O Lord, in your sight.
In ignorance, I have acted impiously,
  worshipping dumb and lifeless idols,
  and I am not worthy to open my mouth to you.
I have sinned, O Lord, before you."

Aseneth admits to her sinful condition, realizing that she has been that way through spiritual ignorance, having had little awareness of what was right or wrong either in her daily or religious life.

"I, Aseneth, the daughter of Pentephres the priest,
  the virgin and queen, once proud and arrogant,
  that once luxuriated in wealth greater than all others,
  am now an orphan, desolate and forsaken by everyone.
With you, Lord, do I seek refuge,
  to you do I bring my petition,
  to you do I call."

Then she presents her petition:

The Wild Primeval Lion Pursues me

"Deliver me from my persecutors
  before I am caught by them.
Just as a little child who is afraid,
  runs to his father and mother,
  and his father, stretching out his arms,
  snatches him up from the ground (*lit.* earth),
  holding him to his breast –
And the child throws his arms around his father's neck,
  and resting upon his father's breast,
  regains his breath and his courage after his fear,
  while the father makes merry
  at his childish trepidation –
So also, Lord, do you stretch out your arms around me
  like a father who loves his child,
  and snatch me up from the Lion."

The "persecutors" or enemies of the soul, as in many of the *Psalms* [50] and much of the ancient mystic literature of the period,[51] are not other people, but the imperfections and passions of the human mind. Once a person begins to realize the extent to which the mind has power over him, through the everyday passions and tendencies that lead the consciousness out into the world, away from the inner reality, then he begins to view these imperfections in a different light. Tendencies of which we were once proud are now perceived as traits and weaknesses to be conquered, like an enemy.

But how to fight successfully against weaknesses such as pride, lust, greed, jealousy, anger, attachment to the world and selfishness is not so obvious. Mystics, ascetics and religious people throughout the world and in all eras have attempted to do so, but with varying degrees of success. Aseneth says that she realizes that she is liable to be overwhelmed by their superior strength. She therefore adopts the approach of a small boy who seeks strength from imagined danger by running into the refuge of his father's arms. She also adds that the source of all these imperfections is the "Lion", replaced in some of the ancient versions of this story by the "earth" or the "supernatural Enemy".

This "Enemy" or "Lion" is the negative power or the devil, to be understood in more modern terminology as the source of the mind and all the entanglements of materiality. The "Enemy" or "Adversary" are common expressions for the devil, found in the canonical gospels as well as in the apocryphal and gnostic literature.[52] The "Lion" is a term more usually found in gnostic texts. It appears, for instance, in the *Gospel of Thomas* as a saying attributed to Jesus:

> Cursed is the man whom the Lion consumes.
>
> *Gospel of Thomas 7, NHS20 pp.56–57*

The metaphor is also associated with the gnostic myth concerning the enslavement of Wisdom in matter.[53] In the *Hypostasis of the Archons,* for instance, the creation of this negative power is described in mythological terms:

> A veil exists between the world above and the realms that are below; and shadow came into being beneath the veil; and that shadow became matter; and that shadow was projected apart.... And it assumed a plastic form moulded out of shadow, and became an arrogant beast resembling a lion.
>
> *Hypostasis of the Archons 94, NHS20 pp.252–53*

In the gnostic text known as the *Pistis Sophia,* Wisdom (personified as the errant soul, *Pistis Sophia*) attempts to enfold this "lion-faced power" because his form of light is enticing and resembles that of the true Light. But she discovers too late that she does not possess the power to do so. Subsequently, she begs the Lord, the "Light of Lights", to help her, because the lion-faced power took away my inner light.

> *Pistis Sophia 32, PS p.47; cf. PSGG p.37*

And in another place she prays:

> You (Lord) will save me
> as I am ensnared by this lion-faced power;
> For you are my Saviour.
>
> *Pistis Sophia 47; cf. PS p.86, PSGG p.70*

Thus, the devil is sometimes referred to as the "lion-faced power", an epithet which would not have been alien to Middle Eastern minds, since many of the pagan and especially Egyptian gods were depicted with the heads of wild beasts.

The expression is encountered in earlier Jewish texts, however, including the *Psalms*,[54] and *Esther* (in her prayer),[55] and these were probably the immediate sources of the metaphor for the author of *Joseph and Aseneth*. In fact, in the myth of the *Pistis Sophia*, her final conquest over the negative power is described as:

> She trampled upon the emanation ... with a lion face.
>
> *Pistis Sophia 66, PS p.141; cf. Psalms 91:13*

And this is immediately related to the meaning of a verse from one of the biblical *Psalms:*

> You (Lord) will tread upon the serpent and basilisk,
> and you will trample upon the lion and dragon.
>
> *Pistis Sophia 67; cf. PS p.143; cf. Psalms 91:13*

The metaphor of the lion is also used explicitly in the pseudo-epigraphic, New Testament letter *1 Peter*, where the unknown writer advises:

Be sober, be vigilant; because your Adversary the devil
    walks about like a roaring lion,
    seeking whom he may devour.

                         1 Peter 5:8; cf. KJV

And likewise in *2 Timothy,* where the writer says:

I was delivered out of the mouth of the Lion.
                2 Timothy 4:17, KJV

Human passions and imperfections were also commonly
described as wild beasts or lions, attempting to devour the
soul.[56] Metaphorically, the king of these passions is the devil.
Consequently, the king of the passions – when they are
depicted as wild animals – is the lion, the king of beasts.
Aseneth therefore continues:

"For behold, the wild, primeval Lion pursues me,
    for he is the father of the gods of the Egyptians,
    and the gods of idol fanatics are his children.
And I have rejected them,
    because they are the Lion's children,
    and I have cast all of them from me and destroyed them,
    and the Lion (*var.* the devil) their father
    is trying to devour me.
"But you, O Lord, rescue me from his hands,
    and deliver me from his mouth,
    lest he snatch me up and tear me to pieces,
    and cast me into the fire of the furnace,
    and the fire cast me into the storm,
    and the storm envelop me in darkness
    and cast me into the depths of the sea,
    and the great Sea Monster
    who existed from the beginning
    should devour me, and I should perish forevermore."

The "wild, primeval Lion", the devil or negative power, pursues all souls, trying to "devour" them. They are devoured in the sense that they are engulfed and lost in the distractions of the senses and the imperfections of the mind. The "Lion" is the "father of gods of the Egyptians" – of all illusion and all false worship. This "Lion" is also "primeval" in the sense that God created him at the very beginning, and he has existed for as long as the creation.

Only the mercy and forgiveness of God can save a soul who is caught by the "Lion" in this world. Otherwise, the soul is cast into body after body in the fiery "furnace", the "storm" or the "darkness" of the physical universe. The material world is compared to a deep sea or abyss, and the devil is thus portrayed as a "great Sea Monster who existed from the beginning". Without the rescuing hand of the Lord, the soul will continue revolving "forevermore" in the labyrinth of the world. Aseneth therefore prays:

Rescue me, O Lord

"Rescue me, O Lord, before all these things befall me.
Rescue me, O Lord, deserted and defenceless,
  for my father and my mother have disowned me, saying,
  'Aseneth is not our daughter,'
    because I destroyed their gods, breaking them to pieces,
    having rejected them.
For this reason, I am now an orphan and deserted,
  and have no other hope save you, O Lord,
    nor any other refuge save your mercy, Friend of man;
Because you are the Father of orphans,
    the Champion of the persecuted,
    and the Helper of those who suffer.
"Have mercy upon me, O Lord, forsaken and orphaned,
    for you alone, O Lord, are a gentle and good father.
For what father is as sweet as you, O Lord?

Who is as quick in mercy as you, O Lord?
Who is as long-suffering towards our sins as you, O Lord?
For behold, all the gifts that my father Pentephres
    has given me as an inheritance
    are transitory and perishable.
But the gifts of your inheritance, O Lord,
    are incorruptible and eternal."

She restates her position and calls on God as the "Friend of man", the "Father of orphans", the "Champion of the persecuted" and the "Helper of those who suffer". God, incarnate as a Son of God, is the only true "Friend of man" because only he can truly help a soul. No other friend in this world, however well-meaning or concerned, can help the soul extricate herself from her entanglements with materiality or help her in the struggle against the mind.

He is a "Father of orphans" because the soul has become lost and homeless in the creation, straying far away from her eternal and real, spiritual home, forgetful of who her real Parent is.

He is a "Champion of the persecuted" because, like a champion who leads an army into war, he fights on behalf of those who trust in him. His disciples are spiritual warriors, and he takes responsibility for guiding them out of the realm of conflict, helping them to defeat the negative power and all obstacles which 'persecute' or trouble them, and stand in their way.

He is a "Helper of those who suffer" in this world by the greatest expedient of all – he takes them out of this world forever, guiding and helping them on the journey back to himself.

Aseneth acknowledges that everything she has in this world is "transitory and perishable", even the wealthy inheritance given to her by her father Pentephres. Only the spiritual gifts of the Divine are "incorruptible and eternal". She therefore continues:

Deliver me from my Ignorance

"Be mindful, then, O Lord, of my low estate,
   and have mercy upon one who suffers.
For behold, Master, I have fled from everything,
   seeking refuge with you, the only Friend of man.
Behold, I have given up all the good things of the earth,
   seeking refuge with you, O Lord,
      dressed in sackcloth and ashes, an orphan and alone.
Behold, I have taken off my royal robe of fine linen,
   of hyacinth interwoven with gold,
      and have put on a black tunic of mourning.
Behold, I have loosed my golden girdle and cast it from me,
   girding myself with a rope and sackcloth.
Behold, I have cast my tiara and my diadem from my head,
   anointing myself with ashes in their stead.
Behold, the floor of my chamber,
   paved with multicoloured and purple stones,
   once sprinkled with oils
   and polished with bright linen cloths,
   is now sprinkled with my tears
   and despoiled by the scattering of ashes.
Behold, O Lord, from the ashes and my tears,
   as much mud has been formed in my chamber
   as on a public highway.
Behold, O Lord, my royal dinner and fatted beasts,
   I have given to stray dogs.
"Behold, O Master,
   seven days and seven nights have I been fasting,
   neither eating bread, nor drinking water.
And my mouth is as dry as the parchment on a drum,
   and my tongue has become like horn,
   and my lips like a potsherd;
And my face has become haggard,
   and my eyes are swollen and disfigured
   from shedding tears;
And all my strength has left me.

"Behold, all the gods whom once I ignorantly worshipped:
    I have recognized that they are dumb and lifeless,
    and I have caused them
    to be trodden under foot by men;
And thieves have made off
    with those that were of silver and of gold,
    and I have sought refuge with you.

"Therefore, O Lord my God,
    do you deliver me from my great ignorance,
    and pardon me.
For, being but a virgin (naive),
    I have fallen unwittingly into error,
    and have spoken calumnies against my lord Joseph,
    because I did not know – wretch that I am –
    that he is your Son.
For wicked men urged me in all sincerity, (saying),
    'Joseph is but the son of a shepherd
    from the land of Canaan.'
And I, wretched one, believed them,
    and fell into Error.
And I despised him, your Elect One,
    and spoke evil of him, not knowing him to be your Son.
For who among men can ever father such beauty,
    and such great wisdom and purity and power
    as is manifest in the all-beautiful Joseph?

"So to you, O Lord, I entrust him,
    for I love him more than my own soul.
Keep him safe in the grace of your Wisdom,
    and give me to him as a maidservant and a slave,
    that I may wash his feet and make his bed,
    and minister to him, and serve him,
    and be a slave to him, all the seasons of my life."

She recounts all that has taken place. Describing her seven-day fast and the resulting condition of her body, she uses the language of divine longing, as in one of the *Psalms:*

> My God, my God, why have you forsaken me?
> The words of my groaning do nothing to save me!
> I call all day, my God, but you never answer,
> all night long, but I get no respite....
>
> My strength is trickling away,
> my bones are all disjointed;
> My heart has turned to wax,
> melting inside me;
> My mouth is as dry as a potsherd,
> and my tongue sticks to my jaws....
>
> I can count every one of my bones,
> while they look on and gloat at me.
> They divide my garments among them
> and cast lots for my clothing.
>
> *Psalms 22:1–2, 14–15, 17–18; cf. KJV, NJB*

The psalmist is speaking of the mystic longing that arises in the soul as she becomes increasingly aware of her separation from the Divine. It is not that God has really deserted the soul, only that the yearning for inner mystic union has swept away all other yearnings as the devotee waits for the longing to be fulfilled. Likewise, with Aseneth when she describes her state of being. She is hoping that God will answer her pleas and come to her, as indeed he soon does, in an unexpected manner.

Aseneth then concludes her prayer with a confirmation of her understanding that Joseph is a Son of God, an Elect One. This is underlined by her description of Joseph's beauty, echoing an earlier passage. Only perfected souls, true Sons of God, possess such beauty. And she asks for the Lord's blessing on her Saviour, once again requesting that she be his "maidservant" and "slave ... all the seasons of my life".

V. The Man of Light

The Chief Captain of the Lord God

The storyteller now describes the answering of Aseneth's prayer:

> When Aseneth had finished making her confession to the
> Lord, behold, the morning star arose in the eastern sky. And
> when Aseneth saw it, she rejoiced, saying, "The Lord God
> has indeed listened to my prayer, for this star is a messenger
> and herald of the light of the great day."
>
> And as Aseneth went on gazing, behold, the heaven near
> the morning star opened and a great and ineffable light
> appeared. And when Aseneth saw it she fell on her face
> upon the ashes; and there came to her from heaven a man
> of light, rays radiating from him. And he stood by her head,
> and called to her, saying, "Aseneth, arise."
>
> And she said, "Who is he that calls me? For the door of
> my chamber is closed and the tower is high: how then has
> he entered my chamber?"
>
> And the man of light called her a second time and said,
> "Aseneth, Aseneth."
>
> And she said, "Here I am, lord. Tell me who you are."
>
> And the man of light said, "I am the chief Captain of the
> Lord God and Commander of all the host of the Most
> High: arise and stand on your feet, and I will tell you what I
> have to say."
>
> And Aseneth raised her head and looked up and saw a
> man, the image of Joseph in every respect, with a robe and a
> crown and a royal staff. But his face was like lightning, and
> his eyes were like sunshine, and the hairs of his head like
> flames of fire. And his hands and his feet like iron shining
> from a furnace, with sparks emanating from his hands and
> feet.

Aseneth meets the spiritual or light form of Joseph. Though, as we have already seen, there are many minor indications that this story was intended as a gnostic parable, the various characteristics of the "man of light" makes this interpretation even more certain. The "man of light" is the "image of Joseph in every respect.... But his face was like lightning, and his eyes were like sunshine, and the hairs of his head like flames of fire. And his hands and his feet like iron shining from a furnace, with sparks emanating from his hands and feet." As far as words permit, this is an accurate description of the astral form of a Master that is met by a disciple on the threshold of the inner planes, or sometimes – as in this instance – even before a disciple really knows anything about the mystic path they are destined to follow. Naturally, such an experience gives a disciple tremendous faith and inspiration.

Reflecting the difficulties in interpreting this and the ensuing passages, scholars have voiced a variety of opinions as to who the "man of light" is supposed to represent, for he does not fit easily into any of the normal, archetypal descriptions of heavenly appearances. In some of the Greek manuscripts and in some translations of this text, the "man of light" has become an "angel" or a "heavenly man", and it is certainly true that there are many angelic appearances described in the ancient texts of Judaism and Christianity to suggest this interpretation. In fact, since this "heavenly man" describes himself as the "chief Captain of the Lord God and Commander of all the host of the Most High", he has often been identified with the archangel Michael of Jewish angelology.

Such a description, however, was also used for the *Logos*, as in an observation of Philo Judaeus, a Hellenistic Jewish philosopher of Alexandria and a contemporary of Jesus. He described the creative Power as being

> God's First-born, the *Logos*, who holds the eldership among the angels, their ruler as it were. And many names are his,

for he is called the 'Beginning' (Source) and the Name of
God, and his *Logos* and the Man-after-the-Image.

    Philo, Confusion of Tongues 28; cf. PCW4 pp.88–91, TGH1 p.233

That an angelic or heavenly being could be understood as a
personification of the *Logos* is likewise reinforced by the
mid-second-century Christian father, Justin Martyr, when
he writes:

> I am now going to give you, my friends, another testimony
> from the scriptures that God before all his other creatures
> begat as the Beginning, a certain spiritual Power proceeding
> from himself, which is called by the Holy Spirit, sometimes
> the Glory of the Lord, and sometimes Son, and sometimes
> Wisdom, and sometimes Angel, and sometimes God, and
> sometimes Lord and *Logos,* and on another occasion he
> calls himself Captain, when he appeared in human form to
> Joshua the son of Nun.
>
> *Justin Martyr, Dialogue with Trypho LXI; cf. OPJG p.20, WJMA p.170*

These extracts also emphasize that the real Master or
Saviour or Son of God is the Word or *Logos*. The *Logos*
manifests at whatever level the soul of the disciple has
reached. At the physical level, he comes as a human being, as
a Master or Saviour; at the astral level, he appears as a
resplendent angel or man of light; and at higher levels, the
Logos appears in a form suited to those higher realms of
creation.

There are some interesting aspects to the description of
the "man of light", partially explained by the author. The
morning star (usually Venus, seen when lying to the west of
the rising sun) symbolizes the coming of light – in this
instance, spiritual light. The author places the star in the
eastern sky, also symbolic of a spiritual dawn. As Aseneth
gazes at the star, the "heaven ... opened" and she sees a
spiritual light, "great and ineffable". Out of this light, the

"man of light" appears. This describes what happens during spiritual practice. A disciple concentrates all his attention at the single eye or eye centre. As the concentration collects at this point, light appears, first as flashes, finally steadying to a constant glow. This may be likened to a sun or a bright star. When the attention is focused on this light, the soul penetrates further within and has her first glimpse of the spiritual or light form of the Master in an angelic or astral form.

As in the description given in *Joseph and Aseneth*, the radiant form resembles the physical form, but is infinitely more beautiful, alluring and full of light. This is why the astral realm is so-called and why the vehicle of the soul in this region is called the astral form or body. It is the mental and spiritual counterpart or blueprint of the physical form. It is 'astral' because it is full of light, shimmering and radiating as if sprinkled with star dust.

The "robe", the "crown" and the "royal staff" are again symbols of the Master's high degree of spirituality. They refer, respectively, to the soul's natural robe of glory or light, to the Master as a spiritual King, and to the Tree of Life or Word which is the essence of a Master, in whatever form he appears.

It is also said that the "man of light" comes and stands by Aseneth's head. She is lying on the floor, of course, so this may have no particular significance. But it could be an allusion to the fact that the spiritual form – though it can also manifest outwardly – is usually seen within the head, in mystic transport, when the attention is withdrawn from the physical senses. That the visitor is no normal earthly man is further underlined by the writer when Aseneth observes that her door is closed and that her upper floor is too high for anyone to have climbed up from the outside.

The "man of light" then greets Aseneth twice, a traditional feature of Jewish writings that depict dialogues between human beings and angelic figures or God himself.

Her New and Brilliant Robe

And, seeing these things, Aseneth fell on her face at his feet, for she was greatly in awe and all her limbs trembled. And the man of light said to her, "Take heart, Aseneth, and fear not, but arise and stand on your feet, and I will tell you what I have to say."

Then Aseneth arose and stood on her feet, and the man of light said to her, "Go immediately to your second chamber and take off the black tunic you are wearing and the sackcloth round your waist, and shake off those ashes from your head, and wash your face and your hands with pure (*var.* living) water. And put on a white, untouched robe, new and glorious, and gird your waist with the bright twin girdle of your virginity. And then return to me, and I will tell you what I have to say."

And Aseneth made haste and went into her second chamber where her treasure chests and ornaments were, and she opened her coffer and took out a white, fine, untouched robe. Then she took off her black tunic of mourning and untied the sackcloth from her waist. And she put on her new and brilliant robe, and girded herself with the bright, twin girdle of her virginity, one girdle around her waist and the other about her breast. And she shook off the ashes from her head, and she washed her hands and her face with pure (*var.* living) water. Then she covered her head with a fine and lovely veil.

Aseneth is told to stand up, to wash herself in "pure" or "living water" (depending on the version), to take off her mourning tunic, to dress in a "white, untouched robe, new and glorious", and to tie two pure "girdles of her virginity" around herself. These are all symbolic of the innately pure state of the soul. Gnostics and mystics of many ages and cultures have described the soul as a diamond, a pearl or a jewel which retains its value even if it becomes dirty by falling into the mud.[57] In some instances, as in *The Virgin,*

the Harlot and the Bridegroom, the soul has also been described as a pure virgin who falls into bad company, becoming
like a prostitute in the profligate way in which her love or
attention is given to the multifarious things and people of
the world. Yet in the end, she regains her virginity and
purity. All these images symbolize the hidden purity of the
soul.

The particular symbolic significance of the twin girdles is
unclear, but the idea is present in allied Judaic literature. In
the gnostic writings of the Mandaeans, the "girdle" is equivalent to the eternal garment, wreath or robe of the soul,
meaning its own pure spirituality,[58] as in:

> Bestir yourselves! Put on your robes!
> Put on your living wreaths, gird on your girdles
>   in which nothing is awry or blemished.
> *Mandaean Prayer Book 67, CPM p.54*

And:

> You, O chosen one, are not from here,
>   from this place you have not been transplanted.
> Your planting, your place was the place of Life,
>   your home the everlasting abode.
> They have set up for you a throne of rest
>   in which there is neither heat nor wrath.
> There is kept for you a girdle
>   in which there is neither trouble nor fault.
> Good one! Rise to the house of Life!
> And go to the everlasting abode!
> They will hang your lamp among lamps of light.
> *Mandaean Prayer Book 92; cf. CPM pp.96–97*

An even closer parallel is found in the *Testament of Job*,
probably of a similar vintage to *Joseph and Aseneth*, where
Job's three daughters are given 'magic' girdles which induce
a change of heart when tied around them, "no longer

minding earthly things". Additionally, they each receive
mystic revelations, described symbolically:

> And she (the first) assumed another heart, no longer
> minding earthly things. And she gave utterance in the
> speech of angels, sending up a hymn to God after the
> pattern of the angels' hymnody; and the Spirit let the
> hymns she uttered be recorded on her robe.
>
> *Testament of Job 48, AOT pp.645–46*

Similarly, the second one, Cassia, on tying on her girdle,

> no longer gave thought to worldly things. And her mouth
> took up the speech of the heavenly powers, and she praised
> the worship of the heavenly sanctuary. So if anyone wants
> to know about the worship that goes on in the heavens, he
> can find it in the hymns of Cassia.
>
> *Testament of Job 49, AOT p.646*

Likewise, the third daughter learns how to praise the "Lord
of Virtues" and the "Father's glory".[59] The singing of hymns
and their recording on a robe may simply be a reflection of
general religious aspirations or they may have been intended
as particular metaphors for listening to the divine Music of
the Word. Either way, Aseneth's twin girdles, as well as her
washing in pure water and her dressing in pure, new clothes,
symbolize her change of heart or her repentance, and her
forthcoming mystic baptism and marriage.

You will be Renewed

> And she returned to the man of light in her first chamber
> and stood before him. And he said to her, "Remove the veil
> from your head, for what reason did you do this? For today
> you are a chaste virgin, and your head resembles that of a
> young man." And Aseneth removed the veil from her head.

Then the man of light said to her, "Take heart, Aseneth, pure virgin, for the Lord has (*var.* I have) heard all the words of your confession and your prayer, and the Lord has (*var.* I have) also seen the self-abasement and suffering of your seven days of abstinence. For behold, from your tears and ashes, much mud has besmeared your face. Therefore, take heart, Aseneth, pure virgin, for behold, your name is written in the Book of Life in heaven among those who were written there from the beginning. Before that of many others was your name written (*var.* by my finger), and it will not be blotted out for all eternity.

"Behold, from today, you will be renewed and refashioned and made alive again, and you will eat the blessed Bread of Life, and drink the blessed Cup of Immortality, and be anointed with the blessed Unction of Incorruption. Take courage, Aseneth, pure virgin, for behold, today I have given you to Joseph for a bride, and he will be your Bridegroom forevermore."

Aseneth is instructed to remove her veil, for she is pure without it. Scholars have pondered over the significance of this. But perhaps it symbolizes the removal of the veils of ego and individuality that surround the soul, and that are removed through the help of a Saviour. Similarly, the symbolic significance of her resemblance to a young man is also obscure. Maybe it signifies that the soul is gradually becoming one with the Saviour.

Aseneth is then told that not only has her prayer been heard, but that she is named in the "Book of Life", and has been so "from the beginning". The "Book of Life" is a common Jewish and Christian concept with origins in the ancient Middle East.[60] It refers to those who are destined for the salvation of eternal life. It was no doubt taken literally by some, but in gnostic and some other texts its meaning is clearly understood metaphorically. In the *Gospel of Truth*, for instance, the "Book of the Living" is even equated with the Word itself.[61] In other places, it is a means of referring to those who have received, or who will receive, initiation into the Word.

This appears to be its intended meaning in the present context. Aseneth has been destined to receive mystic baptism from the very beginning of creation, a statement which also implies the pre-existence of the soul, its immortality and probably the often secret teaching of reincarnation. Many mystics have taught that those souls who are to return to God have been destined to do so from the time of their creation. They have been called the "chosen ones", the "elect" and by many similar names, though the expression has also been claimed by the followers of Judaism and Christianity, and their many sects.

The practical means by which Aseneth's salvation will be effected are also described. She "will eat the blessed Bread of Life, and drink the blessed Cup of Immortality, and be anointed with the blessed Unction of Incorruption." As before, these are all references to mystic baptism into the Creative Word. They are a part of the mystic teaching from which the Christian rituals of the eucharist and external baptism have come into existence by a process of external-ization and literalization. As a result of this blessed contact with the Word of Life, the soul will become the eternal bride of the Word, the divine Bridegroom.

> "Henceforth, no longer will your name be Aseneth, but your name will be 'City of Refuge'. For in you will many nations seek refuge with the Lord God, the Most High, and many peoples will find shelter under your wings. And within your walls will be protected those who, through Repentance, cleave unto God Most High."

Through divine marriage to the *Logos,* Aseneth the soul becomes Aseneth the divine Wisdom. She becomes one with her own Source. She thus becomes the place or "City of Refuge" for all souls who truly repent or turn towards God. The taking of a new name was – and still is – a common practice of those adopting a religious or spiritual path, and the renaming of Aseneth suggests a play on her name. Scholars are undecided, but it is possible that it is based upon an etymology in which Aseneth is derived from a name that means 'ruin'. Thus, from a ruin – a soul lost in the creation – Aseneth has become a City of Refuge. It would certainly make sense.

The mystic literature of all times and places reflects this devotional attitude of self-surrender and of taking refuge or finding "shelter under your wings". In the story, "your wings" are the wings of the Wisdom of God personified as Aseneth. In the *Psalms*,[62] it is God and the Saviour beneath whose wings the devotee seeks shelter:

> I have treasured the words from your lips;
> So that my feet should not slip,
> > my steps never stray from the paths you lay down,
> > from your tracks; ...
> Guard me like the apple of your eye:
> > shelter me in the shadow of your wings.
> > > *Psalms 17:4–5, 8–9; cf. JB, KJV*

And:

> You are my refuge,
> > a strong tower against the enemy.
> Let me stay in your Tent forever,
> > taking refuge in the shelter of your wings.
> > > *Psalms 61:3–4, NJB*

The "man of light" then continues:

Daughter of the Most High

"For Repentance is the daughter of the Most High. And she entreats God Most High at all times on your behalf and for

all who repent, for he is the father of Repentance and she is
the protector of all virgins (pure ones), loving you greatly,
beseeching the Most High for you at all times. And, for all
who repent, she prepares a place of Rest in the heavenly
bridal chamber, and will renew all who repent. And
Repentance is exceedingly beautiful, a virgin pure, gentle
and mild. Therefore God Most High loves her, and all the
angels revere her. And I, too, love her exceedingly, because
she is also my sister. And because she loves you virgins, I
love you, too."

In keeping with Jewish and some early Christian literature,
repentance is personified as an angel or power.[63] It is a way
of expression. Human virtues and divine attributes were
often portrayed in this manner. Repentance is the turning of
the mind and soul towards God. A person has only one
mind and can focus full attention on only one thing at a
time. When the attention of the mind is directed towards
the world and the physical senses, the soul is absorbed in the
play of material life. Mystically, repentance is when the
mind changes its orientation and is directed within: when
the mind and soul are refocused at the single eye, when they
leave the body and begin the journey back to God. Hence,
metaphorically, the man of light describes repentance as he
does. Together with mystic baptism into the Word, it is the
starting point for the soul's return to God.

Interestingly, "Repentance" is portrayed in the same
manner as Wisdom in the biblical Wisdom literature. For
instance, while *Joseph and Aseneth* reads "God Most High
loves her", the *Wisdom of Solomon* has:

> Her (Wisdom's) closeness to God
>   lends lustre to her noble birth,
>   since the Lord of All has loved her.
>   *Wisdom of Solomon 8:3, JB*

Wisdom, as the creative Power, was also called the Mother,[64] for she is the mother or source of all else in creation. Because of this, the gnostics sometimes referred to 'her' as the Virginal Spirit. Thus, because all Masters or Sons of God are emanations of this Power, they can be described as sons of the Virgin, though not in a physical sense. This could also be a part of the origin of the legend of the virgin birth of Jesus.[65]

Since Wisdom is the Power by which true repentance or turning towards the Lord actually becomes a practical possibility, the author may have had some sort of equivalence between the two in mind when describing Repentance in this way. It would certainly make good sense of "Repentance (like Wisdom) is exceedingly beautiful, a virgin pure, gentle and mild." The insistence on Aseneth as a virgin throughout this story would also be given added meaning for, metaphorically speaking, Wisdom or the Word is always and has always been 'virginal', forming the creation without the help of any other Power. The idea also helps elucidate the man of light's comment "she is also my sister". The *Logos* and Wisdom are a related and unified team, like brother and sister, for in reality they are one and the same.

The "heavenly bridal chamber" refers to the higher spiritual realms and also to the eternity of God. There are many uses of this term in Jewish and early Christian literature, especially among gnostic writings.[66]

The Ancient and First Robe

"Now, behold, I am going to Joseph and will tell him everything I have to say concerning you. And he will come to you today, and see you, and rejoice over you and love you, and be your Bridegroom, and you will be a bride to him forevermore.

"So listen to me, Aseneth, pure virgin. Dress in your wedding robe, the ancient and first robe that has been in your chamber from eternity, and wear all your choicest wedding ornaments. Adorn yourself as a good bride and make yourself ready to meet him. For behold, he himself is coming to you today, and when he sees you, he will rejoice."

The man of light concludes by telling Aseneth to dress in her "ancient and first robe that has been in your chamber from eternity" – a reference to the primal and effulgent state of the soul, its immortal "robe of glory", as described in many gnostic texts.

What is your Name, Lord?

And when the man of light had finished speaking these words, Aseneth was overjoyed by all the things that he had said. And falling on her face upon the earth, she made obeisance at his feet, and said to him, "Blessed is the Lord your God the Most High, who sent you out to rescue me from the darkness and to bring me from the depths of the abyss into the light, and blessed is your Name forever. But what is your name, Lord; tell me in order that I may praise and glorify you forevermore."

And the man of light said to her, "My Name is in heaven in the Book of the Most High, written from eternity by the finger of God in the beginning of the book, before all (others), since I am prince of the house of the Most High. And all names written in the Book of the Most High are unutterable, and cannot be heard or seen by a man of this world. For these names are great and wonderful and exceedingly glorious."

Aseneth expresses her gratitude and asks the man of light for his name. He replies that his "Name" underlies all other names in the "Book of the Most High". It was written in this Book by God himself. This unutterable, mystic Name, the Holy Name, which will enable Aseneth to "praise and glorify you forever-more", yet which "cannot be heard or seen by a man of this world", is another designation of the Creative Word. It is by mystic knowledge of this invisible and unutterable Name that the soul can truly know how to worship God.[67] Hence, in the *Acts of Thomas,* when Judas Thomas is asked for the name of his Master Jesus, he replies:

> You are not able to hear his true Name now at this time,
>   but the name that is given to him is Jesus the Messiah.
>
> *Acts of Thomas 8, AAA p.294*

Or as the Coptic *Martyrdom of St Thomas,* a document derived from the *Acts of Thomas,* has it, "you cannot hear his hidden Name".[68]

The "Book of the Most High", that which God has written, is again the Creative Word. All sub-powers or "names", streams of the primal Word, are similarly unutterable and invisible to souls on the material plane. They are all "great and wonderful and exceedingly glorious".

Bring me also a Honeycomb

And Aseneth said, "If I have found favour in your sight, Lord, and can be sure that you will fulfil all the things which you have said to me, then let your maidservant speak to you."

And he said to her, "Speak on."

And she said, "I beg you, Lord, sit down a little upon this bed, because this bed is pure and undefiled, for no other man or woman ever sat upon it. And I will set a table before you, and bring you bread, and you will eat. And, from my storeroom, I will also bring you wine, old and good, the fragrance of which will reach to heaven. And you will drink of it, and thereafter depart upon your way."

And he said to her, "Make haste and bring it quickly."

Aseneth, emboldened by the love and blessing of the man of

light, asks if she may feed him from her storehouse. Again, the symbolism of the "bread" and "wine" is of the Word. The "bread" is the "Bread of Life", as is the "wine, old and good, the fragrance of which will reach to heaven". Wine, Living Wine, the Vine, the First or True Vine, the Fragrance – these are all common metaphors for the creative Power in ancient Middle Eastern mystic literature.[69] It is "wine, old and good" – it is the oldest and sweetest Power in the creation. This is also the natural spiritual food of a Son of God, giving credence to the earlier suggestion that Aseneth's "storehouse" or larder is symbolic of the divine Eternity.

And Aseneth made haste, and set an empty table before him; and as she was starting to fetch bread, the man of light said to her, "Bring me also a honeycomb." And she stood still, and was perplexed and sad because she had no honeycomb in her storeroom. And the man of light said to her, "Why do you stand still?"

And Aseneth said, "My Lord, I will send a boy to the suburbs, because our family estate is nearby. And he will soon bring you a honeycomb from there, and I will set it before you."

But the man of light said to her, "Enter your storehouse and you will find a honeycomb lying on the table. Pick it up and bring it here."

And Aseneth said, "Lord, there is no honeycomb in my storeroom."

He replied, "Go there, and you will find one."

And entering her storeroom, Aseneth found a honeycomb lying on the table; and the comb was large and as white as snow, and full of honey, and the honey was like the Dew of heaven, and the fragrance of it was like the Fragrance (Gk. *pnoe*, also Breath) of Life. And Aseneth marvelled and said within herself, "Did this comb come from the mouth of this man himself? For its fragrance is like the breath of this man's mouth." And Aseneth took the comb, and brought it, and laid it on the table.

And the man of light said to her, "Why is it that you said,

'There is no honeycomb in my house,' and behold, you have brought out a wonderful honeycomb?"

And Aseneth said, "Lord, I never had a honeycomb in my storeroom; but because you spoke, so it has come into being. Has this come out of your mouth? For its fragrance is like the breath of your mouth."

The honeycomb represents the Creative Word. Honey and honeycomb are metaphors commonly associated with the creative Power, as in the *Wisdom of Jesus Ben Sirach,* where Wisdom extends the invitation:

> Come unto me all you that desire me:
>   fill yourselves with my fruits;
> For my memory is sweeter than honey,
>   my inheritance than honeycomb.
>
> *Wisdom of Jesus Ben Sirach 24:19–20; cf. in OPJG p.61*

And similarly in the *Odes of Solomon:*

> Draw for yourselves water
>   from the Living Spring of the Lord,
>   because it has been opened to you.
> Come, all you who thirst, and take a draught,
>   and rest beside the Spring of the Lord.
> For fair it is and pure,
>   and gives rest to the soul.
> Sweeter by far than honey are its waters,
>   and the honeycomb of bees cannot be compared with it;
> Because it flows forth from the lips of the Lord,
>   and from the heart of the Lord is its Name.
>
> And it came unhindered and unseen,
>   but until it sprang up within them,
>   men knew it not.
> Blessed are they who have drunk from it,
>   and have found rest thereby.
>
> *Odes of Solomon 30:1–7, OSD p.134*

Comparing mystic experience of the heavenly realms and
the Word itself to the sweetness of honey stems (at least in
Jud-aism and Christianity) from the *Exodus* allegory, where
the promised land (the eternal realm) is said to flow with
milk and honey:[70]

> I (the Lord) am come down to deliver them
>   out of the hand of the Egyptians (this world);
> And to bring them up out of that land
>   unto a good land and a large,
>   unto a land flowing with milk and honey (eternity).
>
> *Exodus 3:8, KJV*

That the "honey was like the Dew of heaven" makes it clear
that the author is alluding to the "manna" (Bread of Life)
fed to the children of Israel while crossing the desert (the
spiritual aridity of human existence):

> And when the dew that lay was gone up, behold, upon the
> face of the wilderness there lay a small round thing, a s mall
> as the hoar frost on the ground. And when the children of
> Israel saw it, they said one to another, "It is manna (*lit.*
> 'what?')": for they knew not what it was.
>
> And Moses said to them, "This is the bread which the
> Lord has given you to eat." ... And the taste of it (manna)
> was like wafers made with honey.
>
> *Exodus 16:14–15, 31; cf. KJV*

There are many references in Jewish, Christian and allied
literature to "manna" as the "Bread of Life", the "Bread from
heaven" or the Word.[71] In the present story, the honeycomb
is found in Aseneth's own storeroom only through the intervention of the man of light. Aseneth does not realize that
she has it in her own "storeroom" – within herself. It is only
through the grace and blessing of the man of light that she
can find it. Naturally, it is the best of all honeycombs, with a
taste like the "Dew of heaven" – another metaphor for the
Word, as in an explanation of Philo Judaeus:

Do you not see the food of the soul, what it is? It is the *Logos* of God, (raining) continuously like dew, embracing all the soul, suffering no portion to be without part of itself.

But this *Logos* is not apparent everywhere, but only in the man who is destitute of passions and vices; and it is subtle and delicate both to conceive and be conceived, surpassingly translucent and pure to behold.

Philo, *Allegorical Interpretation III:59; cf. PCW1 p.414, TGH1 p.247*

And in the *Odes of Solomon:*

> For the Lord is like the sun,
>   shining upon the face of the land:
> My eyes were enlightened,
>   and my face received the Dew,
>   and my breath (spirit) took pleasure
>   in the pleasant Fragrance of the Lord.
> And he brought me to his paradise,
>   wherein is the abundance of the Lord's pleasure....
> Then I worshipped the Lord because of his glory.
>
> *Odes of Solomon 11:13–17, OSD p.52*

And in *Isaiah:*

> Your dead will come to life, ...
>   awake, exult, all you who lie in the dust.
> Even the dead shall arise,
>   nurtured by the dew of light.
>
> *Isaiah 26:19* [72]

The "dead" addressed by Isaiah are the spiritually dead souls of this world, and there are many other references in mystic literature to this spiritual "dew" or nectar of life. In fact, there is probably no other mystic reality which has been called by as many names as the Word. It indicates the great importance given to it by mystics of all times and places. The writer of *Joseph and Aseneth* certainly makes use of the opportunity to allude to this Power by many of its metaphors, though it may be observed that our author is not particularly subtle or ingenious in the way in which these images are worked into the narrative.

The Word was also called the Breath of God, and the fact that the Fragrance or Breath of the honeycomb is like the "Fragrance" or "breath" from the "mouth" of the man of light once again underlines the essential oneness of the light form of the Saviour with the *Logos*.

This Comb is the Spirit of Life

And the man of light smiled at Aseneth's understanding, and he called her to himself, and stretched out his right hand, and took hold of her head. And Aseneth was astonished by the man of light's hand, because sparks emanated from his hands as from bubbling (*var.* red-hot) iron. And Aseneth gazed fixedly at his hand. And he saw it and smiled, saying, "Blessed are you, Aseneth, because the ineffable mysteries of God Most High have been revealed to you, and blessed are all who cleave to the Lord God in repentance, because they will eat from this Comb. For this Comb is the Spirit of Life. And the bees of the paradise of delight have made this from the Dew of the Roses of Life that are in the paradise of God. And all the angels and the chosen of God and all the sons of the Most High eat of it, because this is a Comb of Life and all who eat of it will never die."

Aseneth is entranced by the vision of the spiritual form, with its emanations of light, seeming like sparks of fire. The man of light now makes the nature of the honeycomb explicit: "This Comb is the Spirit of Life," he says, made by the "bees of the paradise of delight". Underlining the allegorical nature of *Genesis,* the "paradise of delight" is a translation used for the 'garden of Eden' in the *Septuagint,* the Greek version of the Bible extant at that time and used by the writer of this story.

Although *Genesis* makes a clear distinction, Eden itself and the garden of Eden have often been confused and equated. There is "Eden", which symbolizes eternity, and the 'garden planted eastward in Eden' which represents the heavenly realms of creation.[73] In *Joseph and Aseneth*, therefore, the "paradise of delight" and the "paradise of God" could refer to the higher heavenly regions or to eternity itself. Following the prevalent Middle Eastern belief of the times, which spoke of seven heavens, a number of ancient texts identify the garden of Eden with one particular heaven.[74] In this instance, however, the "paradise of delight" and the "paradise of God" seem to refer to the eternity of God.

The man of light also observes that "all the angels and the chosen of God and all the sons of the Most High eat of it, because this is a Comb of Life and all who eat of it will never die". The "chosen of God" and the "sons of the Most High" are those who have been baptized or initiated into the Word. They eat of the "Comb of Life" and "never die". They realize the eternal life of the soul, and never have to return to this world of birth and death. The same idea is found in John's gospel when Jesus says:[75]

This is the bread that comes down from heaven,
    that a man may eat thereof, and not die.
I am the Living Bread that came down from heaven:
    if any man eat of this Bread, he shall live forever.

John 6:50–51; cf. KJV

And again:

Verily, verily, I say unto you, he that hears my Word,
    and believes on him that sent me,
    has everlasting life,
    and shall not come into condemnation;
But is passed from death to life.

John 5:24; cf. KJV

It is clear that the "Living Bread" and the "Comb of Life" are both metaphors for the Word or *Logos*. Coming "into condemnation" refers to rebirth in this world. The soul passes from the death of this world into the eternal life of the Spirit.

> Then the man of light stretched out his right hand and took a small piece from the Comb and ate, and with his own hand placed what was left in Aseneth's mouth, saying to her, "eat", and she ate.
>
> And the man of light said to her, "Behold, now you have eaten the Bread of Life, and have drunk the Cup of Immortality, and been anointed with the Unction of Incorruption. Behold, from today your flesh will flourish like the flowers in the land (*vars.* spring, garden) of the Most High, and your bones will grow strong (*lit.* fat) like the cedars of the paradise of delight of God, and unfailing strength will support you. Accordingly, your youth will not become old age, nor will your beauty ever fail. And you will be like a walled city for all who seek refuge in the Name of the Lord God, the King of Ages."

Aseneth is then given part of the mystic Comb to eat and is told that she will be immortal, forever young and forever beautiful. These are the essential qualities of the pure soul who is always full of vibrant new life and the bliss of true, eternal, spiritual beauty. The writer is weaving together some of the many metaphors associated with the Creative Word and the sense of spiritual peace and bliss that results from contact with it. The comparison of such beauty and well-being to flourishing and flowering plants, for instance, is traditional in Semitic literature. It represents the eternal source of spiritual vigour inherent in the Wisdom of God, of Aseneth transformed into the "City of Refuge". A similar description is found in *Isaiah:*

And the Lord will guide you continually,
  and satisfy your soul in drought,
  and make fat your bones:
And you will be like a watered garden,
  and like a spring of water, whose waters fail not.

Isaiah 58:11; cf. KJV

The "cedars of the paradise of delight of God" are seemingly an allusion to the trees of heaven or paradise, numbered as five in some of the gnostic texts.[76] They refer to the stages of the Creative Word as it passes through the heavenly realms. Following the metaphor of the Word as the Tree of Life (which is also planted in the garden of Eden, according to the *Genesis* story), the trees or "cedars" represent the stages of the Word as it descends, creating the heavenly regions as it goes.

Then the man of light stretched out his right hand and placed his forefinger upon the comb where he had broken it, and it was instantly restored and made whole, becoming complete again, as it had been before. And again the man of light stretched out his hand and, placing his forefinger on the eastern edge of the comb, he drew it across to the western edge, and the track of his finger became like blood. And he stretched out his hand a second time and, placing his finger on the northern edge of the comb, he drew it across to the southern edge, and the track of his finger again became like blood. And Aseneth was standing on his left, watching everything that he was doing.

The man of light makes the sign of the cross upon the comb, and the tracing of his finger appears like blood. This seemingly Christian symbolism may be the interpolation of a later editor. All the same, the cross and the sacrifice or death of Jesus represents the forgiveness of sins which all Masters who are truly incarnations of the *Logos* bring to their disciples. The cross was also used in the mystic symbolism of early Christianity to represent the *Logos*.[77]

And the man of light said to the comb, "Come." And many
bees rose from the cells of that comb, and the cells were
numberless, ten thousand times ten thousand and thousands upon thousands. And the bees were also white like
snow, and their wings like purple and hyacinth, and like
scarlet, and (iridescent) like fine linen woven with gold, and
golden diadems seemed to be upon their heads. And they
also had sharp stings, but would injure no one.

And all these bees encircled Aseneth from head to foot,
while other bees, as large as queens, arose from the cells,
and massed upon her face and her lips, and made a comb
upon her mouth and upon her lips, like the comb that lay
before the man of light. And all the bees ate from the comb
that was upon Aseneth's mouth. And the man of light said
to the bees, "Go now, to your place." At this, all the bees rose
up and flew, and departed to heaven.

The forming of a comb upon the "mouth" of Aseneth by
myriad heavenly bees again represents the transformation
of Aseneth the soul into Aseneth the Wisdom of God. The
bees are the countless souls who dwell in the creation, all of
whom draw their inner life force from the Comb or Spirit of
Life that is formed upon the 'mouth' of Wisdom. The good
souls, those who are in tune with the Wisdom of God, are
sent by the man of light to live in the "fruit-bearing trees"
that grow in the garden of Aseneth, in the garden of Wisdom.
They live in the spiritual realms. It will be recalled that
Aseneth's garden is described earlier in terms reminiscent of
the garden of Eden. Here, the meaning of the symbolism
becomes more apparent. These souls will live on the
heavenly "trees" that are in paradise. They will feed on the
Word of Wisdom.

But as many as wished to injure Aseneth fell to the ground
and died. Thereupon, the man of light stretched his staff
over the dead bees, and said to them, "Arise, too, and depart
unto your place." At which all the dead bees arose, and

departed into the garden that adjoined Aseneth's house, and took up their abode in the fruit-bearing trees.

The souls who wish to injure Aseneth, to turn against Wisdom, they "fell to the ground and died". It means that they fell to the earthly realm at the foot of the creation, entering the world of death, where – spiritually speaking – all souls are as dead. But when the Saviour blesses the souls of this world with his wooden staff – symbolizing the Tree of Life – the souls are restored to life, and they too enter the spiritual realms.

The writer has been piling image upon image in this part of his story and, in case we have missed any of his symbolic meanings, he now draws attention to them when he has the man of light say:

Have you Understood?

And the man of light said to Aseneth, "Have you understood all these things?"

And she said, "Yes, Lord, I have understood all these things."

Then the man of light said to her, "Accordingly, whatever I have spoken to you today will come to pass."

And the man of light, for the third time, stretched out his right hand and touched the side of the comb, and instantly fire arose from the table and consumed the comb, but it did no harm to the table. And much fragrance was emitted from the burning of the comb, and it filled the chamber.

Then Aseneth said to the man of light, "Lord, with me are seven virgins who were brought up with me from my youth, who were born on the same night as myself, and who attend me, and I love them all as sisters. If I will call them, will you bless them too, just as you have blessed me?"

And the man of light said, "Call them." And Aseneth

called the seven virgins and presented them to the man of light. And the man of light said to them, "The Lord God Most High will bless you, and you will be the seven pillars in the City of Refuge, and all the chosen of the city who dwell together will rest upon you, forevermore."

The fire of the comb does no harm, for it is spiritual. Rather its sweet "fragrance" fills the room – quite contrary to the normal smell of burning sugar or honey. Aseneth then asks for her seven companions to be blessed. So the man of light blesses them, designating them the "seven pillars in the City of Refuge, and all the chosen of the city who dwell together will rest upon you, forevermore". This must be a reference to the seven powers who support the seven heavens of creation. There is little doubt as to the author's intended meaning, though his characters are sometimes made to accomplish his ends in a rather somewhat unsubtle manner!

The man of light then said to Aseneth, "Put this table away." And while Aseneth turned away from him, to remove the table, he suddenly vanished from before her eyes, and Aseneth saw something resembling a chariot with four horses, travelling eastward into heaven, and the chariot was like a flame of fire, and the horses like lightning, and the man of light was standing in the chariot.

The man of light then distracts Aseneth's attention so that he can make good his exit and, echoing traditional stories concerning the disappearance of angels and of the ascent of prophets into heaven,[78] he disappears "eastwards", towards the source of light, in a heavenly chariot drawn by four heavenly horses.

Then Aseneth said, "Foolish and rash that I am, the lowly one, for I have spoken with frankness, as if a mere man had come into my chamber, and I knew not that God from heaven had come into it. And now, behold, he returns to heaven, to his place." And she said within herself, "Be gracious, Lord, to your slave, and forgive your maidservant, for in my ignorance, I have spoken rash things before you."

Aseneth then berates herself for having spoken to the man of light as if he had been a mere mortal, not realizing that he was actually God himself. The author wants us to know that the man of light was a manifestation of God. He was the radiant or light form of the Saviour, a spiritual manifestation of the Word or *Logos*.

VI. THE RETURN OF JOSEPH

Her Eyes like the Morning Star

And while Aseneth was still saying these things within herself, behold, a young man, one of the servants of Pentephres, ran in saying, "Behold, Joseph the Powerful One of God, is coming to us today; for his herald is standing at the gates of our garden."

And Aseneth made haste and called her personal retainer, the steward of her house, and said to him, "Make haste, and make my house ready and prepare a fine dinner, for Joseph the Powerful One of God is coming to us today. And when the retainer saw her – her face haggard from the seven days of suffering and weeping and abstinence – he was distressed and wept. And he took hold of her right hand and kissed it tenderly and said, "What ails you, my child, that your face is so haggard?"

And Aseneth said to him, "I have had a very bad headache, and sleep departed from my eyes." And the retainer went away, and prepared the house and the dinner.

And Aseneth remembered the words of the man of light and his instructions, and she made haste and entered her second chamber where the chests containing her ornaments were. And she opened her big coffer and got out her first and ancient robe, her wedding garment, like lightning in appearance, and she put it on. And she girded herself with a girdle of gold and precious stones; and on her hands she put golden bracelets, and upon her feet golden buskins; and around her neck she placed a necklace of great price, hung with innumerable costly stones. And on her head she placed a golden crown, and on the crown, upon her brow, was a large sapphire stone surrounded by six precious stones; and she covered her head with a bride's veil.

Then Aseneth recalled the words of her retainer, telling her that her face was haggard, and she sighed and was much distressed, and said, "Woe is me, the lowly one, for my face is haggard. Joseph will see me and will reject me." So she said to her maidservant, "Bring me pure water from the spring, and I will wash my face." And she brought Aseneth pure water from the spring and poured it into a basin.

And when Aseneth leaned over to wash her face, she saw her own face in the water, shining like the sun. And her eyes were like the morning star as it rises, and her cheeks like the fields of the Most High, and her cheeks were red like pieces of pomegranate, and her lips were a Rose of Life emerging from the bud. Her teeth were set regularly like shield bearers in war, the hair of her head was like the vine that blooms among his fruits in the paradise of God, and her neck as an all-variegated cypress.

And when Aseneth saw herself in the water, she was astonished at the sight and was overjoyed. And she did not wash her face, for she said, "Maybe I will wash off this great and comely beauty."

And the retainer returned to her, saying, "Everything is done as you instructed." But when he looked at her, he was awestruck and lost in wonder, standing enraptured for some time. Then he fell at her feet and began to say, "What is this, my mistress? What is this great and marvellous grace that surrounds you? Has the Lord God of heaven chosen you as a bride for his First-born Son (*var.* his Son Joseph)?"

Joseph now returns and Aseneth makes herself ready to greet him, according to the instructions of the man of light. In the process, she is suddenly transformed from a pale, haggard girl who has been dressed in dark garments, pouring ashes over herself, fasting, and weeping and moaning all week, into a beautiful bride. The change represents the transformation of the soul in human form, drawn and gaunt from its stay in the material universe, into the radiant soul who has been blessed by contact with a Saviour and with the mystic Word of God. The details of the story simply serve to illustrate and emphasize the transformation.

"Her first and ancient robe, her wedding garment, like lightning in appearance" is the soul's natural 'robe of glory'. Likewise, her various ornaments symbolize radiance and beauty of the soul. Her crown, set with seven stones, similarly represents the soul's natural glory, often depicted in other writings of this period as a wreath or garland. The seven stones are probably meant to signify that the pure soul is master of the seven heavens of creation.

The "spring" from which "pure water" is drawn so that she may wash her face is the Living Water of the Word which purifies the soul. In this Water, the soul can see the reflection of her real self and state of being.

The portrayal of Aseneth's beauty is influenced by descriptions of the lover or bride in the biblical *Song of Songs,* where the lover's eyes, cheeks, lips, teeth, hair and neck each convey a particular metaphorical meaning, symbolizing the inherent and natural beauty of the soul. In fact, the resemblance of this description in *Joseph and Aseneth* to that in the *Song of Songs* has developed through successive manuscripts and translations, as editors and translators, realizing the influence, have edited and added to it.

Then, to ensure that we do not miss the meaning, Aseneth's old and faithful servant observes, "Has the Lord God of heaven chosen you as a bride for his First-born Son?" – or, as some manuscripts have it, "for his Son Joseph?".

Joseph Stretched out his Arms

While they were speaking in this manner, a boy came and
said to Aseneth, "Behold, Joseph is standing at the gates to
our garden." Then Aseneth made haste and went down the
stairs from her upper floor with the seven virgins to meet
him, and stood in the verandah of her house. And when
Joseph had entered the garden, the gates were closed and all
strangers remained outside.

As in Joseph's first appearance, the "strangers" are excluded,
implying, perhaps, the absence of all worldliness from the
presence of the Son of the Divine.

And Aseneth came out from the verandah to meet Joseph,
and when he saw her, he marvelled at her beauty, saying to
her, "Who are you? Tell me quickly."

And she said to him, "I am your maidservant Aseneth; all
the idols I have cast away from me, and they were destroyed.
And a man of light came to me today from heaven and gave
me the Bread of Life and I ate, and a Cup of Blessing and I
drank. And he said to me, 'I have given you as a bride to
Joseph, and he will be your bridegroom forevermore. And
your name shall not be called Aseneth, but it will be called
'City of Refuge' and, through you, peoples and kindreds
and families and nations will seek refuge with the Lord God
Most High.'

"And the man of light said to me, 'I will also go to Joseph
and tell him what I have to say concerning you.' And you
will know, lord, whether that man of light has come to you
and whether he has spoken to you concerning me."

Then Joseph said to Aseneth, "Blest are you by the Most
High God and blessed is your name forever, for the Lord
God has laid the foundations of your walls in the Height,
and your walls are adamantine walls of Life, and the sons of
the Living God will dwell in your City of Refuge, and the
Lord God will reign over them forevermore. For that man

of light did come to me today and spoke to me words such as these concerning you. But now, come here to me, pure virgin, why do you stand at a distance from me?"

Then Joseph stretched out his arms and by the beckoning of his eyes called Aseneth. And Aseneth also stretched out her arms and ran to Joseph, and fell on his neck and embraced him, and they entered into the life of the Spirit and were united to one another. And Joseph kissed Aseneth and gave her the Spirit of Life; then he kissed her a second time and gave her the Spirit of Wisdom; then he kissed her a third time and gave her the Spirit of Truth.

Joseph then gives the mystic baptism to Aseneth, symbolized by three kisses. The "Spirit of Life", the "Spirit of Wisdom" and the "Spirit of Truth"[79] are all terms for the Creative Word or *Logos* to whom the soul is retuned at the time of initiation. As before, the "kiss" is a metaphor for the touch of the divine. Here, it symbolizes the spiritual touch of soul to soul at the time of initiation into the Word, as in the *Odes of Solomon:*

> For I have made ready before death comes,
>> and have been sheltered beneath his immortal wings.
> Deathless Life has embraced me,
>> and kissed me;
> And from that Life is the spirit within me,
>> and it cannot die, because it is Life itself.
>
> *Odes of Solomon 28:6–8, OSD pp.124, 126*

So Aseneth receives the Spirit in a mystic initiation, and she enters with Joseph "into the life of the Spirit", and is united with him on the inner spiritual planes.

Your Soul is my Soul

And when they had embraced one another for a long time, intertwining their hands like chains, Aseneth said to Joseph, "Come with me, my Lord, and enter our house, for I have

made ready our house and prepared a fine dinner." And she
took hold of his right hand and led him into her house and
seated him on her father Pentephres' chair, and she brought
water to wash his feet.

And Joseph said, "Let one of the virgins come and wash
my feet."

But Aseneth said to him, "No, Lord, for you are my lord
from this time forward, and I am your maidservant. Why,
therefore, do you say this, that another virgin should wash
your feet? For your feet are my feet, and your hands are my
hands, and your soul is my soul, and no one else will wash
your feet." And she persuaded him, and washed his feet.
And when Joseph looked at her hands, he saw that they
were the Hands of Life, and that her fingers were fine like
the fingers of a skilled scribe. And Joseph took hold of her
right hand and kissed it, and Aseneth kissed his head; and
he seated her at his right hand.

Aseneth now pledges herself to Joseph as she had previously
avowed. She will be both his bride and his maidservant, as
befits the attitude of a disciple. It is likely, too, that a deeper
meaning is implied by Aseneth's declaration that "your feet
are my feet, and your hands are my hands, and your soul is
my soul". For once a disciple has truly surrendered to and
taken refuge in a Master, then the two become one, inwardly
and mystically.

In response, Joseph once again observes that she is a
personification of Wisdom, having the "Hands of Life" and
the "fingers of a skilled scribe", perhaps signifying the
intimate and intricate presence of Wisdom in all things. This
sentence is missing in a number of the manuscripts,
however, and may not be a part of the original story. Either
way, Joseph and Aseneth are mystically united, with Aseneth
seated at Joseph's "right hand", indicative of her pure
spiritual estate. Aseneth's "Hands of Life" and her being
seated at Joseph's "right hand" are also further allusions to
God's creative Power, as we saw earlier.

Then her father and mother and all her family returned from their country estate, and they saw Aseneth as a vision of light, and her beauty as heavenly beauty. And they saw her sitting with Joseph, dressed in a wedding garment. And they were astonished at her beauty, and rejoiced and glorified God who brings life to the dead. And after this, they ate and drank (*var.* and made merry).

Then Pentephres said to Joseph, "Tomorrow, I will call all the noblemen and satraps from throughout the land of Egypt, and will hold a wedding party for you, and you will take my daughter Aseneth for your wife."

But Joseph said, "Not so, for tomorrow I go to Pharaoh the king, because he is like a father to me and has appointed me chief over all this land. And I will speak to him concerning Aseneth, and he will give her to me for my wife."

And Pentephres said to him, "Go in peace."

And Joseph stayed that day with Pentephres, and he knew not Aseneth, for he said, "It is not fitting for a man who worships God to know his wife-to-be before his marriage."

Aseneth's parents return, unaware of all that has been happening in their absence, to find that Joseph and their beloved daughter are to be married. Moreover, they discover that Aseneth has been transformed into a being of heavenly beauty and light, wearing a "wedding garment". This is the pure and innate robe of glory or "garment" of the soul.

So Aseneth's parents "glorified God who brings life to the dead" – the dead being the spiritually dead people of the world who are engrossed in its objects and affairs to the exclusion of their inner spirituality. Here, it is Aseneth who has been raised from the dead through mystic baptism in the Spirit.

Pentephres immediately offers to arrange a grand wedding, but Joseph says that he must first get permission from "Pharaoh the king, because he is like a father to me, and he will give me to her for my wife." In the normal course of events, it is the father of the bride who gives his daughter away. In this instance, Joseph goes to his one and only superior, Pharaoh, who – despite the negative character traditionally assigned to him – seems to symbolize God at this point in the story. In fact, in the *Genesis* story, Pharaoh had previously made Joseph his second-in-command, his chief captain, saying:

> "You shall be overseer in my house, and according to your word shall all my people be ruled. Only in the throne will I be greater than you." And Pharaoh said to Joseph, "See, I have set you over all the land of Egypt." And Pharaoh took his ring from his hand, and put it on Joseph's hand, and arrayed him in vestures of fine linen, and put a gold chain about his neck. And he made him ride in the second chariot that he had; and they cried before him, "Bow the knee." And he made him ruler over all the land of Egypt. And Pharaoh said to Joseph, "I am Pharaoh, and without you no man shall lift up his hand or foot in all the land of Egypt."
>
> *Genesis 41:40–44; cf. KJV*

Interpreted allegorically, Pharaoh is the Lord and Joseph is the *Logos,* the ruler of Egypt, the creation, second only to God, and riding in Pharaoh's "second chariot". This accurately symbolizes the place of the *Logos* in creation, and seems to be the meaning intended.

One wonders, of course, about the remainder of the *Genesis* story of Jacob, Joseph and his eleven brothers. Was it all originally intended to be understood allegorically? The question is too complex to deal with here, but it is noteworthy that in Jewish allegorical commentary on the Bible, of which there is much, it is not considered necessary for *all* of a story to make one complete, watertight and self-consistent allegory. Naturally, it is satisfying when it does, but there are many instances where early commentators like Philo Judaeus, as well as the later Rabbis and Kabbalists knowingly interpret particular aspects of a story out of their original context.

Ancient biblical texts have had a history so hoary and convoluted that there is some justification for this approach. Many biblical books are composite documents, derived from two or more previously independent sources, which have subsequently been exposed to centuries of editorial tampering, rearrangement and frequent misunderstandings and literalizations. Even the original authors would have had their sources and literary influences, perhaps of mystic allegories that they retold, only partially understanding the hidden meaning. At best, therefore, we are only looking at fragments, and the interpretation of small snatches of a story, though seemingly out of context and not always admissible by normal standards, may sometimes be a valid approach.

It seems to be so in this instance, at least in the mind of the author of this allegory. In any event, Pentephres agrees to Joseph's decision, and the writer adds the moralistic comment that it is incorrect for a man and woman to "know" each other before their marriage. This also underlines the fact that the description of their prior union had been meant entirely spiritually.

Joseph therefore goes to Pharaoh and receives permission for his marriage to Aseneth:

Betrothed from Eternity

And Joseph rose early and departed to Pharaoh, and said to him, "Give me Aseneth, daughter of Pentephres, priest of Heliopolis, for my wife."

And Pharaoh said to Joseph, "Behold, has she not been betrothed to you as your wife from eternity? Accordingly, let her be your wife, henceforth and forevermore."

Then Pharaoh sent and called Pentephres, and he came and brought Aseneth and presented her to Pharaoh. And when Pharaoh saw her, he marvelled at her beauty and said,

"The Lord God of Joseph will bless you, my child, and this beauty of yours will remain for all eternity, for the Lord God of Joseph chose you as a bride for him. For Joseph is as the First-born Son of the Most High and you shall be called the daughter of the Lord and his bride, from now and forevermore."

Symbolizing the eternal relationship of the soul and the *Logos*, Pharaoh responds with the observation that the marriage has been destined "from eternity".

Golden Crowns upon their Heads

And after these things, Pharaoh took Joseph and Aseneth and set golden crowns upon their heads, which had been in his house from the beginning and most ancient of times. And Pharaoh set Aseneth at Joseph's right hand and put his hands upon their heads and said, "The Lord God Most High will bless you and will multiply and glorify you unto time eternal." Then Pharaoh turned them round to face one another, and made them draw near, and they kissed each other.

The action now shifts swiftly from the house of Pentephres to Pharaoh's palace. Pharaoh puts "golden crowns upon their heads, which had been in his house from the beginning and most ancient of times", signifying that the union is an ancient one, destined from the beginning of creation. Pharaoh then blesses them and brings them together. The overseer of this divine marriage of the soul with the *Logos* is thus the Lord himself, as the prime Mover in all things.

Crowns or garlands of flowers worn on the head were characteristic adornments of the bride and groom at marriages in ancient times, as they are in many parts of the world today. Like the robe or "wedding garment" of the soul, many mystic writings speak of the soul's crown, wreath or garland.[80] It is another metaphor for the natural, spiritual radiance and beauty of the soul, rediscovered when the soul experiences the divine marriage of mystic union – first with the light form of the Master within, then with the Word from which the Master emanates, and finally with God from whom the Word proceeds. The imagery is encountered, for example, in the very first of the *Odes of Solomon:*

> The Lord is upon my head like a crown of flowers,
> and I shall never be without him.
> A crown of truth has been plaited for me,
> and it has caused thy shoots to grow within me.
> For it is not like a withered crown, which blossoms not:
> but thou art alive upon my head,
> and thou hast blossomed upon me.
> Thy fruits are full and perfect:
> they are full of thy salvation.
>
> *Odes of Solomon 1:1–5, OSD p.12*

Then, concluding the story in conventional fashion, there is a grand wedding feast, lasting a traditional seven days, during which time everybody is forbidden to work, on pain of death:

> And after this Pharaoh arranged a wedding feast for Joseph and a great dinner and there was much rejoicing for seven days. And he called together all the chiefs of Egypt and all the kings of the nations, and issued a proclamation throughout the land of Egypt, saying, "Any man who works during the seven days of Joseph and Aseneth's wedding shall surely die."
>
> And it happened after this, that Joseph knew Aseneth, and Aseneth conceived by Joseph and gave birth to Manasseh and Ephraim his brother in Joseph's house.

The constraint of death echoes the Sabbath restrictions of *Exodus* where anyone who works on the Sabbath is likewise to be "put to death".[81] This may be a simple embellishment of the narrative or it could have a metaphorical meaning, signifying that the entire wedding feast was to be considered as a 'holy day', and that the union was a holy or mystic marriage. Interestingly, neither on the return of Joseph to the house of Pentephres nor at Pharaoh's wedding feast is there any further mention of Joseph's refusal to eat with non-Jews. What was previously appropriate for the sake of the allegory would now cause problems in the flow of the story.

Finally, after the wedding and in deference to the *Genesis* story, Joseph and Aseneth meet as man and wife, and she bears him two children, Manasseh and Ephraim.

VII. Epilogue

I have Sinned, Lord

Following the conclusion of the marriage of Joseph and Aseneth, some manuscripts – including the more ancient Syriac and Armenian translations – append the following psalm. Although the text is uncertain in several places, it is probably a part of the original text. In essence, it is a recapitulation of the story, needing little commentary:

> "I have sinned, Lord,
>> I have sinned in your sight and greatly sinned:
> I, Aseneth, daughter of Pentephres, priest of Heliopolis,
>> of the god who is an overseer of everything.

> "I have sinned, Lord,
>> I have sinned in your sight and greatly sinned:
> For I was at peace in my father's house,
>> but was a boastful and arrogant virgin.

> "I have sinned, Lord,
>> I have sinned in your sight and greatly sinned:
> For I worshipped strange and innumerable gods,
>> and have eaten bread from their sacrifices.

"I have sinned, Lord,
  I have sinned in your sight and greatly sinned:
For I have eaten the bread of strangulation,
  and drunk from the cup of rebellion,
  from the table of death.

"I have sinned, Lord,
  I have sinned in your sight and greatly sinned:
For I knew not the God of heaven,
  nor put my hope in the Most High God of Life.

"I have sinned, Lord,
  I have sinned in your sight and greatly sinned:
For I put my hope in the riches of my (own) splendour,
  and of my beauty I was boastful and arrogant.

"I have sinned, Lord,
  I have sinned in your sight and greatly sinned:
For I despised every man who came before me,
  and no man had value in my eyes.

"I have sinned, Lord,
  I have sinned in your sight and greatly sinned:
For I spurned all who asked my hand in marriage,
  despising and scorning them.

"I have sinned, Lord,
  I have sinned in your sight and greatly sinned:
For I said that there is no prince on earth
  who can loose the girdle of my virginity.

"I have sinned, Lord,
  I have sinned in your sight and greatly sinned:
For I desired to be the bride
  of the great king's (Pharaoh's) first-born son.

"I have sinned, Lord,
  I have sinned in your sight and greatly sinned:
Until Joseph the Powerful One of God came,
  pulling me down from my proud estate,
  humbling me after my arrogance,
  enrapturing me with his beauty,
  catching me with his Wisdom like a fish on a hook,
  and ensnaring me with his Spirit, as a Bait of Life.

"And with his Power, he gave strength to me,
  bringing me to the God of ages.
And through the chief Captain of the Most High,
  he gave me the Bread of Life to eat,
  and the Cup of Wisdom to drink.
And I became a bride to him forevermore."

In the first stanza, the "god who is an overseer of everything" (as the Syriac has it) is probably a reference to the sun. It was commonly thought in the ancient pagan world that the sun-god, from his position high up in the physical heavens, could see everything that went on below. It is an allusion to the name "Heliopolis" which means 'City of the Sun'.

The last two stanzas are a statement of the underlying meaning of the allegory. "Joseph the Powerful One of God" comes and rescues the soul from her condition of sin and selfhood. The soul is pulled down from her "proud estate" and humbled after "her arrogance". She is enraptured with "his beauty" and caught by "his Wisdom like a fish on a hook". She is ensnared by "his Spirit, as a Bait of Life".

The soul is given "strength" by this "Power" and the "chief Captain of the Most High", the *Logos*, gives her the "Bread of Life" and the "Cup of Wisdom". The soul is brought into mystic contact with the Creative Word and becomes "a bride to him forevermore". Such is the age-old mystic path.

NOTES AND REFERENCES

1. *Genesis* 39:21, *KJV.*
2. *Genesis* 37:5*ff.*
3. *Cf.* F. Cumont, *L'Egypte des Astrologues* (Brussels, 1937), pp.127–29. Also *cf. Daniel* 2:1*ff.*, 4:1*ff.*, 5:12, 7:1*ff.*; *Judges* 17:13*ff.*
4. *Cf. Daniel* 1:17; *Deuteronomy* 13:1*ff.*; *Genesis* 20:3*ff.*, 28:11*ff.*, 31:10*ff.*, 31:24*ff.*; *Jeremiah* 23:25–32, 29:8; *Joel* 2:28; *Job* 33:15; *1 Kings* 3:5, 15; *Numbers* 12:6; *1 Samuel* 28:6, 15.
5. *Genesis* 40:1*ff.*
6. *Genesis* 41:1*ff.*
7. *Genesis* 41:42–43, *KJV.*
8. *Genesis* 42:50–52, 46:20.
9. See *Appendix* for further details of the extant manuscripts and the rendering of the story used here.
10. E.W. Brooks, *JA* pp.viii, xviii.
11. *Lit.* 'City of the Sun' (Heb. On), now Materieh, a few miles northeast of Cairo.
12. See *The Wedding Feast*, pp.15–24. See also *e.g. GJ* index: garment; robes; *The Prodigal Son*, in *PSW* p.13; *The Good Samaritan*, in *PSW* pp.18, 21–22; *Adam and Eve*, in *PSW* p.173; *The Robe of Glory*, in *PSW* pp.188–94, *passim.*
13. See *The Damsel of Light*, p.68.
14. *Lit.* 'where her virginity (purity) was protected'.
15. *Lit.* 'court', throughout the text.
16. See *Genesis* 10, where the nations of the world are considered to be derived from the progeny of Noah and his sons, after the flood.
17. *Genesis* 2:8, *KJV.*
18. *Cf. Esther* 8:15.
19. See *The Damsel of Light*, pp.68–69.
20. *E.g. Isaiah* 14:5; *Psalms* 45:6, 110:1; *Wisdom of Solomon* 10:14.
21. See *The Fisher of Souls*, in *PSW* p.131.
22. *Cf. Isaiah* 11:1; *Micah* 7:14; *Psalms* 23:4. See also *e.g.* Manichaean texts: *Manichaean Psalm Book*, *MPB* p.185.
23. *Cf.* in OT: *Deuteronomy* 8:8; *Ezekiel* 16:9, 13, 18–19, 23:41; *Isaiah* 41:19, 61:3; *Joel* 2:19; *Leviticus* 10:7; *Psalms* 23:5, 45:7, 89:20, 92:10, 104:15; *Song of Songs* 1:3.

    In Mandaean texts: *e.g. Mandaean Prayer Book* 23, 24, *CPM* pp.19–20, and many others throughout.

    In Manichaean texts: *e.g. Manichaean Psalm Book* CCXXVIII, CCXXIX, CCXLV, CCLI, CCLVIII, CCLXIII, *MPB* pp.23, 25, 53, 60, 70, 80, 154, 159, 161, 170, 173; *Psalms of Heracleides, Manichaean Psalm Book*, *MPB* pp.191, 193.

    In Nag Hammadi codices: *Dialogue of the Saviour* 130. See also *GJ* index: oil.

See also *Joseph and Aseneth*, p..97; *The Palace of King Gundaphorus*, in *PSW* pp.114–15; *The Good Samaritan*, in *PSW* pp.18–19, 23.

24. *John* 1:14.
25. *Cf. John* 3:27, 6:37–40, 44–46, 65, 10:1–5, 14–15, 27–30, 15:16, 19, 17:1–26; *Matthew* 11:25–27 (in *GJ* pp.678–91).
26. *E.g. Jubilees* 39 (in *e.g. AOT* p.116, *OTP2* pp.128–29); *Testament of the Twelve Patriarchs (Joseph)* 2, 10, 14, 16 (in *e.g. OTP1* pp.819, 821–23).
27. *E.g. Proverbs* 2:16, 5:3, 20, 6:24, 7:5, 22:14, 23:27–28, 33; *Nehemiah* 13:27; *Tobit* 4:12; *Testament of the Twelve Patriarchs (Levi)* 9 (in *e.g. OTP1* p.792).
28. *E.g. Genesis* 24:3, 28:1, 6; *Deuteronomy* 7:3; *Nehemiah* 13:25–29.
29. See *e.g. GJ* index: hell; Sheol.
30. *Cf. Exodus* 29:7, 21, 30:25*ff.*, 37:29, 40:9*ff.*; *1 Kings* 1:39; *2 Kings* 9:3–6; *Leviticus* 8:10*ff.*, 21:10, 12; *1 Samuel* 10:1; *2 Samuel* 16:1–3. See also *Joseph and Aseneth*, pp.89–90.
31. *Babylonian Talmud, Baba Bathra* 172.
32. *Zohar* II:97a.
33. See *e.g. GJ* index: Holy Spirit; Spirit.
34. See *e.g. GJ* index: Life as Word.
35. In many places, the meaning is general, as in the saying, "Everything is in your hands." In other instances, however, it is probably intended to include both. See particularly *Psalms* 21:8, 60:5, 102:25, 138:7.
36. *Manichaean Psalm Book* CCXIX, *MPB* p.2.
37. *Cf. John* 3:27, 6:37–40, 44–46, 65, 10:1–5, 14–15, 27–30, 15:16, 19, 17:1–26; *Matthew* 11:25–27 (in *GJ* pp.678–91).
38. *Cf. Matthew* 11:28–29 (in *GJ* pp.280, 378–79, 955). See also *GJ* index: rest; Rest.
39. *Matthew* 19:21; *Luke* 18:22, 19:8; *Mark* 10:21.
40. In early Christianity, see *GJ* pp.913–53.
41. *2 Baruch* 9:2, 12:5, 20:5, 21:1, 43:3, 47:2 (in *e.g. OTP1* pp.623, 625, 627, 634–35); *4 Ezra* 5:13, 20, 6:31, 35, 9:24–25 (in *e.g. OTP1* pp.532, 535, 545).
42. *Esther* 4:17k*ff.*, *JB* (not in *KJV*).
43. *Lit.* 'hated', and so throughout for 'rejected'.
44. *Lit.* 'come to hate me', and so throughout for 'cast me aside'.
45. *Lit.* 'hates'.
46. *Cf. Matthew* 5:17, *Romans* 8:7, *Wisdom of Jesus Ben Sirach* 15:3 (in *GJ* pp.256–57, 547, 700–1). See also *GJ* index: Law.
47. *E.g. John* 1:1–5, 3:28–30, 5:24–25, 28–29, 6:63, 8:43, 47, 10:2–4, 27–28, 12:30–32, 14:24, 18:37 (in *GJ* pp.234, 292–93, 302–3, 807–8). See also *GJ* index: Voice; Word.
48. *Genesis* 1:1–10.
49. See also *e.g. Psalms* 24:2, 136:6; *2 Enoch* 28:1*ff.*; *2 Peter* 3:5.
50. *E.g. cf. Psalms* 3:7, 5:8, 6:7–8, 7:6, 9:3, 17:9, 18:1, 3, 37, 40, 48, 21:8, 23:5, 25:2, 19 *etc.*

51. See *e.g. GJ* index: enemies.
52. *E.g. Matthew* 13:18–19, 28, 37–39 (in *GJ* pp.373–74, 700, 983–85). See also *GJ* index: Adversary; Enemy.
53. *E.g. Pistis Sophia* 30–32, 35, 39, 47–48, 50, 52–55, 66–67, 75–78, 102 (in *e.g. PS* p.43 *etc.*); *Apocryphon of John* 10 (in *e.g. NHL* p.110); *On the Origin of the World* 100 (in *e.g. NHS21* pp.34–35).
54. *Cf. Psalms* 7:2, 10:9, 17:12, 22:13, 21, 35:17, 57:4, 58:6, 91:13.
55. *Esther* 4:17k*ff.*, JB (not in *KJV*).
56. *E.g. Psalms,* as above. See also *GJ* index: beasts, wild *or* savage.
57. *E.g. Gospel of Philip* 62, in *e.g. The Robe of Glory,* in *PSW* p.204.
58. See also *Mandaean Prayer Book* 67, 70, 182, 208, 210, *CPM* pp.53–54, 57, 163, 176–79.
59. *Testament of Job* 50, *AOT* p.646.
60. *E.g. Luke* 10:20; *Acts of John* XVII (in *e.g. ANT* p.261); all in *GJ* pp.694–97. See also *Book of Revelation* 3:5 (in *GJ* pp.414–15), 13:18, 20:15, 21:27, 22:19; *Exodus* 32:32–33; *Psalms* 87:6; *Jubilees* 30:22–23 (in *e.g. AOT* p.95, *OTP2* p.114); in the Dead Sea Scrolls: *cf. War Scroll* (1QM) XII (in *e.g. CDSS* p.175); *Words of the Heavenly Lights* (4Q504) VI (in *e.g. CDSS* p.366). See also *The Robe of Glory,* in *PSW* pp.191, 219, 221. See also *GJ* index: Book of Life.
61. *Gospel of Truth* 19–20 (in *e.g. GS* pp.254–56, *GT* pp.56–62, 66–70, 78, *NHL* pp.41–42; in *GJ* pp.696–97).
62. See also *Psalms* 63:7–8, in *Joseph and Aseneth,* pp.101–2.
63. *E.g. 1 Enoch* 40:9 (in *e.g. AOT* p.224, *OTP1* p.32); *Shepherd of Hermas, Visions* 5:7 (in *e.g. AF2* p.71). See also *Testament of the Twelve Patriarchs (Gad)* 5:7 (in *e.g. OTP1* p.815).
64. See *e.g. GJ* index: Mother.
65. For a full discussion, see *GJ* pp.651–57.
66. *E.g. Chaldaean Breviary, BCB* 1:407, 3:425 (in *MEM* p.116, *GJ* p.849); *Nestorian Liturgies, NR2* XLI p.196 (in *GJ* p.753). In Manichaean texts: *Manichaean Psalm Book* CCXLIX, CCLIII, CCLXI, CCLXIII, CCLXIV, CCLXXXI *etc.* (in *e.g. MPB* 58, 63–64, 75–76, 79–81, 102, 117, 193, 197, *GJ* pp.848–49).
67. See *e.g. GJ* index: Name.
68. *Martyrdom of St Thomas, MAA* p.96 (in *GJ* p.269).
69. See *e.g. GJ* index: First, Vine; fragrance; Vine; Wine.
70. See also *Exodus* 3:17, 13:5, 33:3.
71. *E.g. Book of Revelation* 2:7 (in *GJ* p.414); *John* 6:32–35, 47–51 (in *GJ* p.248); *Nehemiah* 9:15; *Psalms* 105:40. See also *GJ* index: manna; Bread.
72. *JB,* together with a translation from an unpublished lecture by Rabbi Jerry Steinberg, in *HN* p.114.
73. *Genesis* 2:8. See also *Adam and Eve,* in *PSW* pp.160–61.
74. *E.g.* in the Judaic text, *3 Baruch* 4:8 (in *e.g. OTP1* p.666), the Tree of the Knowledge of Good and Evil is located in the third heaven.

75. See also *John* 8:51, 11:26.
76. *E.g. Gospel of Thomas* 19 (in *NHS20* pp.60–61, *GJ* p.360); *Second Book of Jeu* 50 (in *BC* p.119, *GJ* p.717). See also *GJ* (Five Trees: pp.359–61, 586, 713–14, 716).
77. See *e.g. GJ* index: cross.
78. *E.g.* Elijah's ascent in *1 Kings* 2:11; the angel's ascent in *Judges* 6:21, 13:20–22.
79. **Spirit(s) of Truth:** *cf. John* 14:17, 15:26, 16:13 (in *GJ* pp.823–25); *1 John* 4:6 (in *GJ* pp.529–30, 700); *Jubilees* 25:14 (in *e.g. OTP2* p.105); *Shepherd of Hermas, Mandates* 3:4 (in *e.g. AF2* p.75); *Testament of the Twelve Patriarchs (Judah)* 20:5 (in *e.g. OTP1* p.800). In the Dead Sea Scrolls: *Community Rule (1QS)* III:18*ff.*, IV:21, 23 (in *e.g. CDSS* pp.101, 103); *War Scroll (1QM)* XIII:10 (in *e.g. CDSS* p.177).

    Spirit of Life: *Romans* 8:2 (in *GJ* p.402); *Apocalypse of Adam* 66 (in *e.g. NHS11* pp.158–61, *GJ* p.265); *Apocryphon of John* 25–27 (in *e.g. NHL* pp.119–20, *GJ* p.432); Irenaeus, *Against Heresies* III:XI.8, quoting *1 Timothy* 3:15 (in *e.g. AH1* p.293, *GJ* p.66).
80. See *e.g. GJ* index: garland; wreath.
81. *Exodus* 35:2.

APPENDIX

The Text of *The Virgin, the Harlot and the Bridegroom*

Though the place of composition is unknown, the content of the text tells us something of the author's background. He is either well-versed in the Jewish scriptures or he has an anthology of 'proof texts' to refer to, perhaps both. His Bible is the *Septuagint*, the Greek translation made under the aegis of Ptolemy I (c.367–283 BC, successor to Alexander the Great in Egypt) during the third and second centuries BC, and used by Jews throughout the Hellenized world in ancient Middle Eastern and Mediterranean countries. He is also familiar with the Christian gospels, including John, as well as the letters of Paul, and he speaks of Jesus as the "Saviour".

His range of citations, drawn from the socio-religious milieu of his immediate environment, demonstrates his universal approach to the understanding of gnostic or mystic truth. However, since he starts and ends his selection of quotations with those from Jewish texts, it may be presumed that either he or his intended audience, or both, were more familiar with the Jewish scriptures than with any other. All the same, he presents the gnostic teaching in a simple way that either Jews, Christians or pagans would readily understand. 'Pagan', it might be observed, is the term used to designate anyone who does not or did not profess

Judaism, Christianity or Islam. In the Graeco-Roman Middle East of two thousand years ago, this included everyone from the Greek philosophers such as Pythagoras, Plato and their later followers, to believers in the pantheon of Greek, Roman, Egyptian and other gods.

The writer's quotations help to put a date to his composition. His use of Jesus' sayings, for instance, places him in the Christian era. Although many of the sayings attributed to Jesus would have been extant in other forms, prior to their incorporation into the gospels of Mark, Matthew and Luke, and could have been found there, the author also quotes from the narrative material of these gospels. Since it is commonly accepted that these gospels were composed no earlier than 65 AD, this provides us with an earliest date for the writing of the story. The writer also quotes from John's gospel, the major part of which is generally reckoned to have been written even later in the first century. This helps to date *The Virgin, the Harlot and the Bridegroom* to no earlier than the beginning of the second century. The author also speaks of Paul and the apostles in a way that presupposes that they had not recently passed away. In fact, from this and other evidence, the treatise is generally believed by scholars to have been written towards the end of the second century, around 200 AD.[1]

The Text of Joseph and Aseneth

From a study of its content, scholars are generally agreed that *Joseph and Aseneth* was written before 200 AD by someone with a background in Hellenistic Judaism, that is, Judaism as practised in the Hellenized, Greek-speaking world outside Palestine. The author's Bible, for example, was the *Septuagint*, the Greek translation used by Jews and early Christians throughout the Hellenized world. It has also been pointed out that the character of *Joseph and Aseneth* is not too far removed from Jewish *midrash*, a rich style of biblical commentary using stories, parables and so on. Certainly, there are many passages in the text which indicate that the writer was at least familiar with, if not steeped in, biblical as well as apocryphal writings of the period, and much of the style is borrowed from such texts. But there are also elements of Hellenistic, as well as Judaic, romance woven into the story.

Some of the motifs, however, such as the Bread of Life and the Cup of Immortality, are seemingly Christian in character or were at least in vogue during early Christian times, though their origin was in Greek and Jewish literature. Since the story can be viewed as the 'conversion' of Aseneth by Joseph, it is often presumed that it was written to encourage 'conversion' to Judaism – and was later edited to provide a Christian flavour. But there are a number of difficulties with this point of view, not the least of which is that the supposed Christianizations are actually an integral part of the narrative, and cannot easily be accounted for as the work of a later editor. Moreover, the Judaism depicted in the story is significantly different from that taught by the traditional schools of Judaism of those times.

The text, then, would seem to be a *potpourri* of influences, reflecting the international character of the period, and there are few, if any, metaphors and themes in *Joseph and Aseneth* that can be considered truly original. A possibility, therefore, which makes good sense of all this data, is that the original text was indeed written by someone with a Hellenistic Jewish background at a time when terminology associated with early Christianity was in common use. The writer, however, was someone of a gnostic disposition who saw essential spiritual truths in both Judaism and Christianity. His outlook was thus more universal than that of an adherent to either conventional Judaism or Christianity. There have been universally minded, spiritual people at every turn in history, however sectarian, divisive and parochial the general atmosphere of the times may have been.

The earliest extant text would seem to be a sixth-century Syriac translation from the Greek, though the story probably receives its earliest-surviving mention in the late fourth century.[2] The earliest extant Greek manuscript is tenth century. Nevertheless, scholars are fairly confident in dating the original text to before 200 AD. Some have even suggested that it originated as early as the second century BC. If the suggestion is correct that the text is not a later Christian overworking of an earlier Jewish text,[3] then its origin must have been during the first two centuries AD – a time when gnosticism reached a peak.

About seventy manuscripts of *Joseph and Aseneth* survive. Sixteen are in Greek, the remainder being translations of the Greek into various languages. But with the exception of the Syriac, all these manuscripts date from the tenth century or later. With regard to the actual dates of translation, again with the exception of the Syriac, only the original Armenian can be assigned an early date, probably to the sixth or seventh centuries. At the present time, forty-five Armenian manuscripts exist, of varying character and usefulness. But all were transcribed many centuries after the original Armenian translation.

The sixteen Greek manuscripts fall into four main groups, known to scholars as *a, b, c* and *d*. Group *d* represents a much condensed version, with many omissions, and made no later than the eleventh century. Group *a* originated from a revision made no later than the tenth century to modernize the ancient biblical Greek. Group *c* stems from a late medieval or early modern revision. And group *b* contains the fullest and most widely distributed version of the text, and is probably closer to the original than the other three. Most of the translations, including the Syriac, the Armenian and two *circa* thirteenth-century Latin versions, are also closer to this fourth group than to any of the others. Only the *circa* fifteenth-century Slavonic text is different, showing more in common with the condensed *d* than any other version.

The relationship between all these texts has never been fully explored and a number of English translations exist, based upon different manuscripts and groups of texts, and expressing different scholarly opinions concerning the details. Four of these are the most significant. There is a 1901 translation of the Armenian made by Jacques Issaverdens *(UWOT);* a 1918 translation of the Greek by E.W. Brooks *(JA)* based largely on manuscripts from group *a* with reference to the various translations where deemed appropriate; a 1985 translation of the condensed Greek version (group *d*) by D. Cook (in *AOT*); and a 1985 translation by C. Burchard (in *OTP2*) that largely favours readings from group *b*, but seems in many places to be a modernization of E.W. Brooks' translation of group *a*.

The present rendering is a collation of these four texts with a preference for the longer readings of group *b* (C. Burchard) and the Greek of group *a* (E.W. Brooks). In fact, the textual variants, though of interest from a scholarly point of view, do not usually create a conflict of meaning, and the emphasis in this rendering has focused on clarity of the English. If any significant editing of the original text took place, it happened before any of these manuscripts came into existence and is now largely untraceable. For the interested English reader, details of the ancient texts themselves can be found in the introductions and footnotes to the four English translations, those of Burchard having proved particularly useful for the present commentary.

Ancient Greek literary style commonly introduced sentence after sentence with an 'and', rarely varying the style. Although it adds to the ancient flavour of the text when conveyed in translation, it can become obtrusive to modern tastes when used to excess. A more liberal spread of alternatives has therefore been employed, as well as the restructuring of sentences and the choosing of alternative vocabulary, here and there. The antiquated English of E.W. Brooks, derived from the *King James Version* of the Bible and still in vogue in his day for the translation of ancient religious texts, has also been modernized in most instances. Care, of course, has been taken to preserve the essential meaning, and any variants among the different texts and translations, significant for their spiritual meaning, have been noted in brackets, preceded with a '*var.*'.

NOTES AND REFERENCES

1.   W.C. Robinson, *NHS21* pp.136.
2.   *Pilgrimage of Etheria* (*c.* 382 AD); in *On Holy Places*, Peter the Deacon of Monte Cassino, tr. in *UJA* p.137, tr. in *OTP2* p.187.
3.   See *Joseph and Aseneth*, p.75.

ABBREVIATIONS

See *Bibliography* for full details

AAA	*Apocryphal Acts of the Apostles*, W.R. Wright
AF1–2	*The Apostolic Fathers*, 2 vols., tr. Kirsopp Lake
AH1–2	*Against Heresies*, 2 vols., Irenaeus, tr. A. Roberts and W.H. Rambaud
ANT	*The Apocryphal New Testament*, M.R. James
AOT	*The Apocryphal Old Testament*, ed. H.E.D. Sparks
BC	*The Books of Jeu and the Untitled Text in the Bruce Codex*, tr. V. MacDermot
BCB	*Breviarium Chaldaicum*, 3 vols., P. Bedjan
BSOAS	*Bulletin of the School of Oriental and African Studies*
CDSS	*The Complete Dead Sea Scrolls in English*, tr. G. Vermes
CH	*Clementine Homilies*, tr. T. Smith *et al.*
CPM	*The Canonical Prayerbook of the Mandaeans*, tr. E.S. Drower
CTPD	*The Complete Text of the Pahlavi Dinkard*, Part I-II, ed. D.M. Madan
DP1–4	*The Dialogues of Plato*, 4 vols., tr. B. Jowett
GJ	*The Gospel of Jesus: In Search of His Original Teachings*, John Davidson
GS	*The Gnostic Scriptures*, B. Layton
GSR	*Gnosis on the Silk Road*, H.-J. Klimkeit
GT	*The Gospel of Truth*, K. Grobel
GVM	*The Great Vohu Manah and the Apostle of God*, G. Widengren
HO	*The Odyssey*, Homer, tr. E.V. Rieu
HN	*The Holy Name: Mysticism in Judaism*, Miriam Caravella
JA	*Joseph and Asenath*, E.W. Brooks
JB	*Jerusalem Bible* (1966)
KJV	*Authorized King James Version*

KRPH	*The Kabbalah or the Religious Philosophy of the Hebrews*, Adolphe Franck, tr. I. Sussnitz
LXX	*Septuagint* (C3rd BC Greek translation of the Bible)
MAA	"Mythological Acts of the Apostles", A.S. Lewis
MEM	"Mesopotamian Elements in Manichaeism", G. Widengren
MHCP	*The Manichaean Hymn-Cycles in Parthian*, M. Boyce
MJR1–8	*The Mathnawi of Jalalu'ddin Rumi*, 8 vols., R.A. Nicholson
ML	*Manichaean Literature*, J.P. Asmussen
MM1–3	"Mitteriranische Manichaica aus Chinesisch-Turkestan", 3 vols., F.C. Andreas and W.B. Henning
MPB	*A Manichaean Psalm-Book*, Part II, ed. and tr. C.R.C. Allberry
MT	Masoretic Text (traditional Hebrew text of the Jewish Bible)
NHL	*The Nag Hammadi Library in English*, ed. J.M. Robinson
NHS11	*Nag Hammadi Studies* XI: *Nag Hammadi Codices V,2–5 and VI*, ed. Douglas M. Parrot
NHS20	*Nag Hammadi Studies* XX: *Nag Hammadi Codex II,2–7*, vol. 1, ed. Bentley Layton
NHS21	*Nag Hammadi Studies* XXI: *Nag Hammadi Codex II,2–7*, vol. 2, ed. Bentley Layton
NHS28	*Nag Hammadi Studies* XXVIII: *Nag Hammadi Codices XI, XII, XIII*, ed. Charles W. Hedrick
NHS30	*Nag Hammadi Studies* XXX: *Nag Hammadi Codex VII, XIII*, ed. Birger A. Pearson
NJB	*The New Jerusalem Bible* (1985)
NR1–2	*The Nestorians and Their Rituals*, 2 vols., G.P. Badger
OPJG	*The Origin of the Prologue to St John's Gospel*, J.R. Harris
OSD	*The Odes of Solomon: Mystical Songs from the Time of Jesus*, John Davidson
OT	The Old Testament
OTP1–2	*The Old Testament Pseudoepigrapha*, 2 vols., ed. J.H. Charlesworth
PCW1–10	*Philo*, 10 vols., tr. F.H. Colson and G.H. Whitaker
PS	*Pistis Sophia*, tr. V. MacDermot
PSGG	*Pistis Sophia, A Gnostic Gospel*, G.R.S. Mead
PSW	*The Prodigal Soul: The Wisdom of Ancient Parables*, John Davidson
RAH	*Refutation of All Heresies*, Hippolytus, tr. S.D.F. Salmond
RMP	*A Reader in Manichaean Middle Persian and Parthian*, M. Boyce

RSV	*The Holy Bible: Revised Standard Version* (1952)
SBEG	*The Secret Books of the Egyptian Gnosis,* J. Doresse
SP	"Sadwes and Pesus", Mary Boyce
TGH1–3	*Thrice-Greatest Hermes,* 3 vols., G.R.S. Mead
UJA	"Untersuchungen zu Joseph und Aseneth", C. Burchard
UWOT	*The Uncanonical Writings of the Old Testament Found in the Armenian Mss. of the Library of St Lazarus,* tr. J. Issaverdens
WAF	*The Writings of the Apostolic Fathers,* tr. A. Roberts *et al.*
WJMA	*The Writings of Justin Martyr and Athenagoras,* tr. M. Dods

BIBLIOGRAPHY

All texts referenced in the present book are listed, plus a few others of related interest. Subsections include both primary sources as well as studies, commentaries and so on. Editions referenced in the text are the ones listed below. Dates of first publication have been added in square brackets where significant. Books and articles are listed by their title, rather than by author or translator – in a selection such as this, it makes them easier to find. For a more complete bibliography, see The Gospel of Jesus *(John Davidson, 1995, rev. edn., 2004).*

Apocryphal Literature (Christian and Jewish)

The Apocrypha and Pseudoepigrapha of the Old Testament in English, 2 vols., R.H. Charles; Oxford University Press, Oxford, 1913.

The Apocryphal Acts of the Apostles, tr. W.R. Wright; Williams and Norgate, Edinburgh, 1871.

Apocryphal Gospels, Acts, and Revelations, tr. A. Walker; T. & T. Clark, Edinburgh, 1870.

The Apocryphal New Testament, tr. M.R. James; Oxford University Press, Oxford, 1989 [1924].

The Apocryphal New Testament: A Collection of Apocryphal Christian Literature in an English Translation based on M.R. James, ed. J.K. Elliott; Oxford University Press, Oxford, 1993.

The Apocryphal Old Testament, ed. H.E.D. Sparks; Oxford University Press, Oxford, 1985.

The Clementine Homilies, tr. T. Smith *et al.;* T. & T. Clark, Edinburgh, 1870.

The Clementine Recognitions, tr. T. Smith; T. & T. Clark, Edinburgh, 1867.

Joseph and Asenath, E.W. Brooks; SPCK, London, 1918.

The Life and Confession of Asenath the Daughter of Pentephres of Heliopolis, M. Brodrick; Philip Wellby, London, 1900.

"The Mythological Acts of the Apostles", A.S. Lewis; in *Horae Semiticae* IV (1904), C.J. Clay, London.

New Testament Apocrypha, 2 vols., E. Hennecke, ed. W. Schneemelcher, tr. R.McL. Wilson; Westminster, Philadelphia, Pennsylvania, 1963–64.

The Odes and Psalms of Solomon, J.R. Harris; Cambridge University Press, Cambridge, 1911.

The Odes and Psalms of Solomon, 2 vols., J.R. Harris and A. Mingana; Longmans, Green and Company, London, 1920.

"The Odes of Solomon", tr. J.A. Emerton, in *The Apocryphal Old Testament*, ed. H.E.D. Sparks; Oxford University Press, Oxford, 1985.

The Odes of Solomon, tr. J.H. Bernard; Cambridge University Press, Cambridge, 1912.

The Odes of Solomon, tr. J.H. Charlesworth; Oxford University Press, Oxford, 1973.

The Odes of Solomon: Mystical Songs from the Time of Jesus, John Davidson; Clear Books, Bath, 2004.

The Old Testament Pseudoepigrapha, 2 vols., ed. J.H. Charlesworth; Darton, Longman and Todd, London, 1983.

The Uncanonical Writings of the Old Testament Found in the Armenian Mss. of the Library of St Lazarus, tr. J. Issaverdens; Armenian Monastery of St Lazarus, Venice, 1901.

"Untersuchungen zu Joseph und Aseneth", C. Burchard; in *Wissenschaftliche Untersuchungen zum Neuen Testament* 8 (1965), Tübingen.

Bibles

The Holy Bible: Authorized King James Version [1611]; Oxford University Press, Oxford.

The Holy Bible: New Revised Standard Version; Oxford University Press, New York, 1989.

The Holy Bible: Revised Standard Version; Oxford University Press, Oxford, 1952.

The Jerusalem Bible; Darton, Longman and Todd, London, 1966.

The New Jerusalem Bible; Darton, Longman and Todd, London, 1985.

Christianity

Against Heresies, Irenaeus; in *The Writings of Irenaeus*, 2 vols., tr. A. Roberts and W.H. Rambaud; T. & T. Clark, Edinburgh, 1868–69.

The Apostolic Fathers, 2 vols., tr. Kirsopp Lake; William Heinemann, London, 1912–13.

The Apostolic Fathers: An American Translation, E.J. Goodspeed; Harper and Brothers, New York, 1950.

Breviarium Chaldaicum, 3 vols., P. Bedjan; Leipzig, 1886–87.

An Early Christian Philosopher: Justin Martyr's Dialogue with Trypho, Chapters One to Nine, J.C.M. van Winden; E.J. Brill, Leiden, 1971.

Fragment of an Uncanonical Gospel from Oxyrhynchus, B.P. Grenfell and A.S. Hunt; Oxford University Press, London, 1908.

The Gospel of Jesus: In Search of His Original Teachings, rev. edn., John Davidson; Science of the Soul Research Centre, New Delhi and Clear Books, Bath, UK, 2004 [1995].

Light on Saint John, Maharaj Charan Singh; Radha Soami Satsang Beas, Punjab, India, 1985.

Light on Saint Matthew, Maharaj Charan Singh; Radha Soami Satsang Beas, Punjab, India, 1978.

The Nestorians and Their Rituals, 2 vols., G.P. Badger; Joseph Masters, London, 1852.

New Sayings of Jesus and the Fragment of a Lost Gospel, B.P. Grenfell and A.S. Hunt; Henry Frowde, London, 1904.

The Origin of the Prologue to St John's Gospel, J.R. Harris; Cambridge University Press, Cambridge, 1917.

The Oxford Companion to the Bible, ed. B.M. Metzger and M.D. Coogan; Oxford University Press, Oxford, 1993.

The Oxford Dictionary of the Christian Church, rev. edn. F.L. Cross and E.A. Livingstone; Oxford University Press, Oxford, 1983.

The Oxyrhynchus Logia and the Apocryphal Gospels, C. Taylor; Oxford University Press, Oxford, 1899.

The Parables of Jesus, R.W. Funk *et al.;* Polebridge, Sonoma, California, 1990.

Refutation of All Heresies, Hippolytus, tr. S.D.F. Salmond; T. & T. Clark, Edinburgh, 1868.

The Sayings of Our Lord: From an Early Greek Papyrus, B.P. Grenfell and A.S. Hunt; Henry Frowde, London, 1897.

The Writings of the Apostolic Fathers, tr. A. Roberts *et al.;* T. & T. Clark, Edinburgh, 1867.

The Writings of Justin Martyr and Athenagoras, tr. M. Dods *et al.;* T. & T. Clark, Edinburgh, 1867.

The Writings of Tatian and Theophilus and the Clementine Recognitions, tr. B.P. Pratten *et al.;* T. & T. Clark, Edinburgh, 1867.

Gnosticism

The Acts of Thomas: Introduction, Text, Commentary, A.F.J. Klijn; E.J. Brill, Leiden, 1962.

The Books of Jeu and the Untitled Text in the Bruce Codex, tr. V. MacDermot; E.J. Brill, Leiden, 1978.

Fragments of a Faith Forgotten, G.R.S. Mead; Health Research, Mokelumne Hill, California, 1976 [1906].

The Gnostic Gospels, E. Pagels; Random House, New York, 1979.

The Gnostic Scriptures, B. Layton; SCM, London, 1987.

The Gospel According to Thomas, tr. A. Guillaumont *et al.;* E.J. Brill, Leiden, 1959.

The Gospel of Truth, K. Grobel; Adam and Charles Black, London, 1960.

The Hymn of Jesus, tr. G.R.S. Mead; Watkins, London, 1963 [1907].

The Hymn of the Soul, tr. A.A. Bevan; Cambridge University Press, Cambridge, 1897.

The Hymn of the Soul contained in the Syriac Acts of Thomas, ed. & tr. A.A. Bevan; Cambridge University Press, Cambridge, 1897.

The Nag Hammadi Library in English, ed. J.M. Robinson; E.J. Brill, Leiden, 1988.

Nag Hammadi Studies XI: *Nag Hammadi Codices V,2–5 and VI,* ed. Douglas M. Parrott; E.J. Brill, Leiden, 1979.

Nag Hammadi Studies XX: *Nag Hammadi Codex II,2–7,* vol. 1, ed. Bentley Layton; E.J. Brill, Leiden, 1989.

Nag Hammadi Studies XXI: *Nag Hammadi Codex II,2–7,* vol. 2, ed. Bentley Layton; E.J. Brill, Leiden, 1989.

Nag Hammadi Studies XXII: *Nag Hammadi Codex I (the Jung Codex),* vol. 1, ed. Harold W. Attridge; E.J. Brill, Leiden, 1985.

Nag Hammadi Studies XXIII: *Nag Hammadi Codex I (the Jung Codex),* vol. 2, ed. Harold W. Attridge; E.J. Brill, Leiden, 1985.

Nag Hammadi Studies XV: *Nag Hammadi Codices IX and X,* ed. Birger A. Pearson; E.J. Brill, Leiden, 1981.

Nag Hammadi Studies XXVIII: *Nag Hammadi Codices XI, XII, XIII,* ed. Charles W. Hedrick; E.J. Brill, Leiden, 1990.

Nag Hammadi Studies XXX: *Nag Hammadi Codex VII, XIII,* ed. Birger A. Pearson; E.J. Brill, Leiden, 1996.

Pistis Sophia, tr. G. Horner; SPCK, London, 1924.

Pistis Sophia, tr. V. MacDermot; E.J. Brill, Leiden, 1978.

Pistis Sophia: A Gnostic Gospel, G.R.S. Mead; Garber Communications, New York, 1984 [1921].

The Prodigal Soul: The Wisdom of Ancient Parables, John Davidson;
Clear Books, Bath, 2004.

The Robe of Glory, John Davidson; Element, Shaftesbury, UK, 1992.

The Secret Books of the Egyptian Gnosis, J. Doresse; Inner Traditions,
Rochester, Vermont, 1986.

The Teachings of Silvanus, J. Zandee; Nederlands Instituut voor het
Nabije Oosten, Leiden, 1991.

Greek and Roman

The Dialogues of Plato, 4 vols., tr. B. Jowett; Oxford University Press,
Oxford, 4th edn. 1953 [1871].

The Odyssey, Homer; tr. E.V. Rieu, rev. D.C.H. Rieu; Penguin,
London, 1991 [1946].

Plato (Euthyphro, Apology, Crito, Phaedo, Phaedrus), tr. H.N. Fowler;
William Heinemann, London, 1966.

Thrice-Greatest Hermes, 3 vols., G.R.S. Mead; Theosophical Publish-
ing Society, London, 1906.

Judaism

The Complete Dead Sea Scrolls in English, tr. G. Vermes; Penguin,
London, 1998.

The Holy Name: Mysticism in Judaism, M.B. Caravella; Radha Soami
Satsang Beas, Dera Baba Jaimal Singh, Punjab, 1989.

The Kabbalah or the Religious Philosophy of the Hebrews, Adolphe
Franck, tr. I. Sussnitz; University Books, New York, 1967.

Philo, 10 vols., tr. F.H. Colson and G.H. Whitaker; William
Heinemann, London, 1941.

The Song of Songs: The Lover and the Divine Beloved, John
Davidson; Clear Books, Bath, 2004.

The Works of Philo Judaeus, 4 vols., tr. C.D. Yonge; H.G. Bohn,
London, 1855.

Who Wrote the Bible? R.E. Friedman; Jonathan Cape, London, 1988.

Mandaeanism

The Canonical Prayerbook of the Mandaeans, tr. E.S. Drower;
E.J. Brill, Leiden, 1959.

The Gnostic John the Baptizer, G.R.S. Mead; John Watkins, London,
1924.

Das Johannesbuch der Mandäer, M. Lidzbarski; Alfred Töpelmann, Giessen, 1915.

The Mandaeans of Iran and Iraq, E.S. Drower; Oxford University Press, Oxford, 1937.

Mandäische Liturgien, M. Lidzbarski; Weidmannsche Buchhandlung, Berlin, 1920.

The Secret Adam, E.S. Drower; Oxford University Press, Oxford, 1960.

Manichaeism

Gnosis on the Silk Road: Gnostic Texts from Central Asia, H.-J. Klimkeit; Harper, San Francisco, 1993.

The Great Vohu Manah and the Apostle of God, G. Widengren; Uppsala, Sweden, 1945.

"Handschriften-Reste in Estrangelo-Schrift aus Turfan, Chinesisch-Turkistan", F.W.K. Müller; in *Sitzungsberichte Preussischen Akademie der Wissenschaften*, Berlin, 1904, pp.348–52.

Handschriften-Reste in Estrangelo-Schrift aus Turfan, Chinesisch-Turkistan II, F.W.K. Müller; Berlin, 1904; also in *Abhandlungen der Königlich Preussischen Akademie der Wissenschaften*, 1904.

Mani and Manichaeism, G. Widengren; Weidenfeld and Nicholson, London, 1961.

The Manichaean Hymn-Cycles in Parthian, tr. M. Boyce; Oxford University Press, London, 1954.

Manichaean Literature, J.P. Asmussen; Scholars' Facsimiles and Reprints, Delmar, New York, 1975.

A Manichaean Psalm-Book, Part II, ed. & tr. C.R.C. Allberry; Kohlhammer, Stuttgart, 1938.

"Mesopotamian Elements in Manichaeism", G. Widengren; in *Uppsala Universitets Arsskrift* 3 (1946), University of Uppsala, Sweden.

"Mitteriranische Manichaica aus Chinesisch-Turkestan", 3 vols., F.C. Andreas and W.B. Henning; in *Sitzungsberichte der Königlich Preussischen Akademie der Wissenschaften* (1932, 1933, 1934), Berlin.

A Reader in Manichaean Middle Persian and Parthian, M. Boyce; E.J. Brill, Leiden, 1975.

"Sadwes and Pesus", Mary Boyce; in *BSOAS* 13 (1951), University of London.